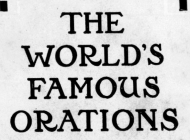

THE
WORLD'S
FAMOUS
ORATIONS

WILLIAM JENNINGS BRYAN
EDITOR-IN-CHIEF

FRANCIS W. HALSEY
ASSOCIATE EDITOR

IN TEN VOLUMES

Vol. IX
AMERICA—II

FUNK and WAGNALLS COMPANY
New York and London

The World's Famous Orations

VOL. IX

AMERICA—II

1818–1865

CONTENTS

Vol. IX—America—II (1818-1865)

[1] Otherwise known as "The Seventh of March Speech."

CONTENTS

VOL. IX

AMERICA—II

1818-1865

HAYNE

ON THE FOOTE RESOLUTION[1]

(1830)

Born in 1791, died in 1840; United States Senator from South Carolina in 1823–32; Governor of South Carolina in 1832–34.

SIR, let me tell the gentleman that the South repudiates the idea that a pecuniary dependence on the federal government is one of the legitimate means of holding the States together. A monied interest in the government is essentially a base interest: and just so far as it operates to bind the feelings of those who are subjected to it, to the government—just so far as it operates in creating sympathies and interests that would not otherwise exist—is it opposed to all

[1] Hayne was the first man to put forth conspicuously the doctrine of Nullification, by which was meant the right of a State to arrest the operation of a law of Congress, provided the State in convention should decide that the law was unconstitutional. The speech from which passages are here given was delivered in the Senate on January 21, 1830, and is the one to which Webster made his famous reply on January 26. Webster had already made a speech on the Foote resolution, so that Hayne's speech was a reply to Webster, as Webster's second speech was a reply to Hayne. Abridged. The following is the text of the resolution:

"Resolved, that the Committee on Public Lands be instructed to inquire and report the quantity of public lands remaining unsold within each State and Territory, and whether it be expedient to limit for a certain period the sales of the public lands to such lands only as have heretofore been offered for sale and are now subject

3

the principles of free government, and at war with virtue and patriotism. Sir, the link which binds the public creditors, as such, to their country, binds them equally to all governments, whether arbitrary or free. In a free government this principle of abject dependence, if extended through all the ramifications of society, must be fatal to liberty. Already have we made alarming strides in that direction. The entire class of manufacturers, the holders of stocks, with their hundreds of millions of capital, are held to the government by the strong link of pecuniary interests; millions of people—entire sections of country, interested, or believing themselves to be so, in the public lands and the public treasure, are bound to the government by the expectation of pecuniary favors.

If this system is carried much farther, no man can fail to see that every generous motive of attachment to the country will be destroyed; and in its place will spring up those low, grov-

to entry at the minimum price. And also, whether the office of surveyor-general and some of the land offices may not be abolished without detriment to the public interest; or whether it be expedient to adopt measures to hasten the sale and extend more rapidly the surveys of the public lands."

Samuel A. Foote, the author of this resolution, was a United States senator from Connecticut (1827-1833). The effect of the resolution had been to arouse among senators from the West a belief that it was intended as a scheme to check migration to the West, thus hindering the growth of that section for the benefit of New England and other older sections of the North. Southern senators for similar reasons opposed it, but they also believed that Northern senators desired by this measure to limit public revenues and to centralize the government.

eling, base and selfish feelings which bind men to the footstool of a despot by bonds as strong and enduring as those which attach them to free institutions. Sir, I would lay the foundation of this government in the affections of the people—I would teach them to cling to it by dispensing equal justice, and above all, by securing the "blessings of liberty" to "themselves and to their posterity."

We are ready to make up the issue with the gentleman, as to the influence of slavery on individual and national character—on the prosperity and greatness, either of the United States or of particular States. Sir, when arraigned before the bar of public opinion, on this charge of slavery, we can stand up with conscious rectitude, plead not guilty, and put ourselves upon God and our country. Sir, we will not consent to look at slavery in the abstract. We will not stop to inquire whether the black man, as some philosophers have contended, is of an inferior race, nor whether his color and condition are effects of a curse inflicted for the offenses of his ancestors. We deal in no abstractions. We will not look back to inquire whether our fathers were guiltless in introducing slaves into this country. If an inquiry should ever be instituted in these matters, however, it will be found that the profits of the slave-trade were not confined to the South. Southern ships and Southern sailors were not the instruments of bringing slaves to the shores of America, nor did our merchants reap the profits of that "accursed traffic."

But, sir, we will pass over all this. If slavery, as it now exists in this country, be an evil, we of the present day found it ready made to our hands. Finding our lot cast among a people whom God had manifestly committed to our care, we did not sit down to speculate on abstract questions of theoretical liberty. We met it as a practical question of obligation and duty. We resolved to make the best of the situation in which providence had placed us, and to fulfil the high trusts which had devolved upon us as the owners of slaves, in the only way in which such a trust could be fulfilled without spreading misery and ruin throughout the land. We found that we had to deal with a people whose physical, moral and intellectual habits and character totally disqualified them from the enjoyment of the blessings of freedom. We could not send them back to the shores from whence their fathers had been taken; their numbers forbade the thought, even if we did not know that their condition here is infinitely preferable to what it possibly could be among the barren sands and savage tribes of Africa; and it was wholly irreconcilable with all our notions of humanity to tear assunder the tender ties which they had formed among us, to gratify the feelings of a false philanthropy.

What a commentary on the wisdom, justice, and humanity of the Southern slave-owner is presented by the example of certain benevolent associations and charitable individuals elsewhere! Shedding weak tears over sufferings which had existence only in their own sickly imaginations, these "friends of humanity" set themselves systematically to work to seduce the slaves of the South from their masters. By means of missionaries and political tracts, the scheme was in a great measure successful. Thousands of t se deluded victims of fanaticism were seduced into the enjoyment of freedom in our Northern cities. And what has been the consequence? Go to these cities now and ask the question. Visit the dark and narrow lanes, and obscure recesses which have been assigned by common consent as the abodes of those outcasts of the world—the free people of color. Sir, there does not exist on the face of the whole earth a population so poor, so wretched, so vile, so loathsome, so utterly destitute of all the comforts, conveniences, and decencies of life, as the unfortunate blacks of Philadelphia, and New York and Boston. Liberty has been to them the greatest of calamities, the heaviest of curses.

Sir, I have had some opportunities of making comparison between the condition of the free negroes of the North and the slaves of the South, and the comparison has left not only an indelible impression of the superior advantages of the latter, but has gone far to reconcile me to slavery itself. Never have I felt so forcibly that touching description, "The foxes have holes, and the birds of the air have nests, but the Son of Man hath not where to lay his head," as when I have seen this unhappy race, naked and houseless, almost starving in the streets, and abandoned by all the world. Sir, I have seen, in the neighborhood of one of the most moral, religious and refined cities of the North, a family of free blacks driven to the caves of the rocks, and there obtaining a precarious existence from charity and plunder.

When the gentleman from Massachusetts adopts and reiterates the old charge of weakness as resulting from slavery, I must be permitted to call for the proof of those blighting effects which he ascribes to its influence. I suspect that when the subject is closely examined, it will be found that there is not much force even in the plausible objection of the want of physical power in slave-holding States. The power of a country is compounded of its population and its wealth, and in modern times, where, from the very form and structure of society, by far the greater portion of the people must, even during the continuance of the most desolating wars, be employed in the cultivation of the soil and other peaceful pursuits, it may be well doubted whether slave-holding States, by reason of the superior value of their productions, are not able to maintain a number of troops in the field fully equal to what could be supported by States with a larger white population, but not possesed of equal resources.

It is a popular error to suppose that in any possible state of things the people of a country could ever be called out *en masse,* or that a half, or a third, or even a fifth part of the physical force of any country could ever be brought into the field. The difficulty is not to procure men, but to provide the means of maintaining them; and in this view of the subject it may be asked whether the Southern States are not a source of strength and power and not of weakness to the country—whether they have not contributed, and are not now contributing largely to the wealth and prosperity of every State in this Union. From a statement which I hold in my hand it appears that in ten years —from 1818 to 1827, inclusive—the whole amount of the domestic exports of the United States was $521,811,045. Of this, three articles (the product of slave labor)—viz., cotton, rice, and tobacco—amounted to $339,203,232, equal to about two-thirds of the whole. It is not true, as has been supposed, that the advantages of this labor are confined almost exclusively to the Southern States. Sir, I am thoroughly convinced that at this time the States north of the Potomac actually derive greater profits from the labor of our slaves than we do ourselves. It appears from our public documents that in seven years, from 1821 to 1827 inclusive, the six Southern States exported $190,-337,281, and imported only $55,646,301. Now the difference between these two sums (near

$140,000,000) passed through the hands of the Northern merchants, and enabled them to carry on their commercial operations with all the world. Such part of these goods as found its way back to our hands came charged with the duties, as well as the profits of the merchant, the ship-owner, and a host of others, who found employment in carrying on these immense exchanges; and for such part as was consumed in the North we received in exchange Northern manufactures charged with an increased price to cover all the taxes which the Northern consumer has been compelled to pay on the imported article. It will be seen, therefore, at a glance how much slave labor has contributed to the wealth and prosperity of the United States, and how largely our Northern brethren have participated in the profits of that labor.

There is a spirit which, like the father of evil, is constantly "walking to and fro about the earth, seeking whom it may devour": it is the spirit of false philanthropy. The persons whom it possesses do not indeed throw themselves into the flames, but they are employed in lighting up the torches of discord throughout the community. Their first principle of action is to leave their own affairs, and neglect their own duties, to regulate the affairs and duties of others. Theirs is the task to feed the hungry and clothe the naked of other lands, while they thrust the naked, famished, and shivering beggar from their own doors—to instruct the heathen while their own children want the bread of life.

When this spirit infuses itself into the bosom of a statesman (if one so possessed can be called a statesman), it converts him at once into a visionary enthusiast. Then it is that he indulges in golden dreams of national greatness and prosperity. He discovers that "liberty is power," and, not content with vast schemes of improvement at home which it would bankrupt the treasury of the world to execute, he flies to foreign lands to fulfil obligations to "the human race," by inculcating the principles of "political and religious liberty," and promoting the "general welfare" of the whole human race. It is a spirit which has long been busy with the slaves of the South and is even now displaying itself in vain efforts to drive the government from its wise policy in relation to the Indians. It is this spirit which has filled the land with thousands of wild and visionary projects which can have no effect but to waste the energies and dissipate the resources of the country. It is the spirit of which the aspiring politician dexterously avails himself when, by inscribing on his banner the magical words, Liberty and Philanthropy, he draws to his support that class of persons who are ready to bow down at the very name of their idols.

But, sir, whatever difference of opinion may exist as to the effect of slavery on national wealth and prosperity, if we may trust to ex-

11

perience, there can be no doubt that it has never yet produced any injurious effect on individual or national character. Look through the whole history of the country from the commencement of the Revolution down to the present hour; where are there to be found brighter examples of intellectual and moral greatness than have been exhibited by the sons of the South? From the Father of his Country down to the distinguished chieftain who has been elevated by a grateful people to the highest office in their gift,[1] the interval is filled up by a long line of orators, of statesmen, and of heroes, justly entitled to rank among the ornaments of their country, and the benefactors of mankind. Look at "the Old Dominion," great and magnanimous Virginia, "whose jewels are her sons." Is there any State in this Union which has contributed so much to the honor and welfare of the country? Sir, I will yield the whole question—I will acknowledge the fatal effects of slavery upon character, if any one can say that for noble disinterestedness, ardent love of country, exalted virtue, and a pure and holy devotion to liberty, the people of the Southern States have ever been surpassed by any in the world.

The senator from Massachusetts tells us that the tariff is not an Eastern measure, and treats it as if the East had no interest in it. The senator from Missouri insists it is not a Western

---

[1] Andrew Jackson.

measure, and that it has done no good to the West. The South comes in, and in the most earnest manner represents to you that this measure, which we are told "is of no value to the East or the West," is "utterly destructive of our interests." We represent to you that it has spread ruin and devastation through the land and prostrated our hopes in the dust. We solemnly declare that we believe the system to be wholly unconstitutional and a violation of the compact between the States and the Union; and our brethren turn a deaf ear to our complaints, and refuse to relieve us from a system "which not enriches them, but makes us poor indeed." Good God! Mr. President, has it come to this? Do gentlemen hold the feelings and wishes of their brethren at so cheap a rate that they refuse to gratify them at so small a price? Do gentlemen value so lightly the peace and harmony of the country that they will not yield a measure of this description to the affectionate entreaties and earnest remonstrances of their friends? Do gentlemen estimate the value of the Union at so low a price that they will not even make one effort to bind the States together with the cords of affection? And has it come to this? Is this the spirit in which this government is to be administered? If so, let me tell gentlemen the seeds of dissolution are already sown, and our children will reap the bitter fruit.

What, sir, was the conduct of the South during the Revolution? Sir, I honor New England for her conduct in that glorious struggle. But great as is the praise which belongs to her I think at least equal honor is due to the South. They espoused the quarrel of their brethren with a generous zeal which did not suffer them to stop to calculate their interest in the dispute. Favorites of the mother country, possessed of neither ships nor seamen to create a commercial rivalship, they might have found in their situation a guaranty that their trade would be forever fostered and protected by Great Britain. But trampling on all considerations either of interest or of safety, they rushed into the conflict, and fighting for principle, periled all in the sacred cause of freedom. Never was there exhibited in the history of the world higher examples of noble daring, dreadful suffering, and heroic endurance than by the Whigs of Carolina during the Revolution. The whole State, from the mountains to the sea, was overrun by an overwhelming force of the enemy. The fruits of industry perished on the spot where they were produced, or were consumed by the foe. The "plains of Carolina" drank up the most precious blood of her citizens! Black and smoking ruins marked the places which had been the habitations of her children! Driven from their homes into the gloomy and almost impenetrable swamps, even there the spirit of liberty survived, and South Carolina (sustained by the example of her Sumters and her Marions) proved by her conduct that tho the soil might be overrun, the spirit of her people was invincible.

I come now to the War of 1812—a war which I well remember was called in derision (while its event was doubtful) the Southern War, and sometimes the Carolina War, but which is now universally acknowledged to have done more for the honor and prosperity of the country than all other events in our history put together. What, sir, were the objects of that war? "Free trade and sailors' rights!" It was for the protection of Northern shipping and New England seamen that the country flew to arms. What interest had the South in that contest? If they had sat down coldly to calculate the value of their interests involved in it, they would have found that they had everything to lose and nothing to gain. But, sir, with that generous devotion to country so characteristic of the South, they only asked if the rights of any portion of their fellow citizens had been invaded; and when told that Northern ships and New England seamen had been arrested on the common highway of nations, they felt that the honor of their country was assailed; and acting on that exalted sentiment "which feels a stain like a wound," they resolved to seek in open war for a redress of those injuries which it did not become freemen to endure.

Sir, the whole South, animated as by a common impulse, cordially united in declaring and promoting that war. South Carolina sent to your councils, as the advocates and supporters of that war, the noblest of her sons. How they fulfilled that trust let a grateful country tell. Not a measure was adopted, not a battle fought, not a victory won which contributed in any degree to the success of that war to which Southern councils and Southern valor did not largely contribute.

It will be recollected, sir, that our great causes of quarrel with Great Britain were her depredations on Northern commerce and the impressment of New England seamen. From every quarter we were called upon for protection. Importunate as the West is now represented to be on another subject, the importunity of the East on that occasion was far greater. I hold in my hands the evidence of the fact. Here are petitions, memorials, and remonstrances from all parts of New England, setting forth the injustice, the oppression, the depredations, the insults, the outrages committed by Great Britain against the unoffending commerce and seamen of New England, and calling upon Congress for redress.

Well, sir, the war at length came, and what did we behold? The very men who had been for six years clamorous for war, and for whose protection it was waged, became at once equally clamorous against it. They had received a miraculous visitation; a new light suddenly beamed upon their minds, the scales fell from their eyes, and it was discovered that the war was declared from "subserviency to France"; that Congress, and the executive, "had sold themselves to Napoleon"; that Great Britain had, in fact, "done us no essential injury"; that she was "the bulwark of our religion"; that where "she took one of our ships, she protected twenty"; and that if Great Britain had impressed a few of our seamen, it was because "she could not distinguish them from her own." And so far did this spirit extend that a committee of the Massachusetts Legislature actually fell to calculation, and discovered to their infinite satisfaction, but to the astonishment of all the world beside, that only eleven Massachusetts sailors had ever been impressed.

Never shall I forget the appeals that had been made to the sympathies of the South, in behalf of the "thousands of impressed Americans" who had been torn from their families and friends, and "immured in the floating dungeons of Britain." The most touching pictures were drawn of the hard condition of the American sailor, "treated like a slave," forced to fight the battles of his enemy, "lashed to the mast, to be shot at like a dog." But, sir, the very moment we had taken up arms in their defense, it was discovered that all these were mere "fictions of the brain"; and that the whole number in the State of Massachusetts was but eleven; and that even these had been "taken by mistake." Wonderful discovery! The secretary of state had collected authentic lists of no less than six thousand impressed Americans. Lord Castlereagh[1] himself acknowledged sixteen hundred. Calculations on the basis of the number found on board of the *Guerriere,* the *Macedonian,* the *Java,* and other British ships (captured by the skill and gallantry of those heroes whose achievements are the treasured monuments of their country's glory), fixed the number at seven thousand; and yet, it seems, Massachusetts had lost but eleven! Eleven Massachusetts sailors taken by mistake! A cause of war, indeed! Their ships, too, the capture of which had threatened "universal bankruptcy," it was discovered that Great Britain was their friend and protector; "where she had taken one, she had protected twenty." Then was the discovery made that subserviency to France, hostility to commerce, "a determination on the part of the South and West to break down the Eastern States," and especially (as reported by a committee of the Massachusetts Legislature) "to force the sons of commerce to populate the wilderness," were the true causes of the war.

But let us look a little further into the conduct of the peace party of New England at that important crisis. Whatever difference of opinion might have existed as to the causes of the war, the country had a right to expect that when once involved in the contest, all America

---

[1] British foreign secretary, 1812–1822.

would have cordially united in its support. Sir, the war effected in its progress a union of all parties at the South. But not so in New England; there, great efforts were made to stir up the minds of the people to oppose it. Nothing was left undone to embarrass the financial operations of the government, to prevent the enlistment of troops, to keep back the men and money of New England from the service of the Union—to force the president from his seat. Yes, sir, "the island of Elba! or a halter!" were the alternatives they presented to the excellent and venerable James Madison.

Sir, the war was further opposed by openly carrying on illicit trade with the enemy, by permitting that enemy to establish herself on the very soil of Massachusetts, and by opening a free trade between Great Britain and America with a separate custom-house. Yes, sir, those who can not endure the thought that we should insist on a free trade in time of profound peace, could without scruple claim and exercise the right of carrying on a free trade with the enemy in a time of war; and finally, by getting up the renowned "Hartford Convention," [1] and preparing the way for an open resistance to the government, and a separation of the States. Sir, if I am asked for the proof of those things I fearlessly appeal to contemporary history, to the public documents of the country,

[1] Its sessions, held in secret, lasted from December 15, 1814, until January 5, 1815.

to the recorded opinion and acts of public assemblies, to the declaration and acknowledgments, since made, of the executive and Legislature of Massachusetts herself.

As soon as the public mind was sufficiently prepared for the measure, the celebrated Hartford Convention was got up; not as the act of a few unauthorized individuals, but by authority of the Legislature of Massachusetts; and, as has been shown by the able historian of that convention, in accordance with the views and wishes of the party of which it was the organ. Now, sir, I do not desire to call in question the motives of the gentlemen who composed that assembly—I knew many of them to be in private life accomplished and honorable men, and I doubt not there were some among them who did not perceive the dangerous tendency of their proceedings. I will even go further and say that if the authors of the Hartford Convention believed that "gross, deliberate, and palpable violations of the Constitution" had taken place, utterly destructive of their rights and interests, I should be the last man to deny their rights to resort to any constitutional measures for redress. But, sir, in any view of the case, the time when, and the circumstances under which that convention assembled, as well as the measures recommended, render their conduct, in my opinion, wholly indefensible.

Who, then, Mr. President, are the true friends of the Union? Those who would confine the federal government strictly within the limits prescribed by the Constitution; who would preserve to the States and the people all powers not expressly delegated; who would make this a federal and not a national Union, and who, administering the government in a spirit of equal justice, would make it a blessing and not a curse. And who are its enemies? Those who are in favor of consolidation—who are constantly stealing power from the States and adding strength to the federal government. Who, assuming an unwarrantable jurisdiction over the States and the people, undertake to regulate the whole industry and capital of the country. But, sir, of all descriptions of men, I consider those as the worst enemies of the Union who sacrifice the equal rights which belong to every member of the Confederacy to combinations of interested majorities, for personal or political objects.

Thus, it will be seen, Mr. President, that the South Carolina doctrine is the republican doctrine of '98—that it was promulgated by the fathers of the faith—that it was maintained by Virginia and Kentucky in the worst of times— that it constituted the very pivot on which the political revolution of that day turned—that it embraces the very principles, the triumph of which at that time saved the Constitution at its last gasp, and which New England statesmen were not unwilling to adopt, when they believed themselves to be the victims of unconstitutional legislation. Sir, as to the doctrine that the federal government is the exclusive judge of the extent as well as the limitations of its powers, it seems to me to be utterly subversive of the sovereignty and independence of the States. It makes but little difference, in my estimation, whether Congress or the Supreme Court is invested with this power. If the federal government, in all or any of its departments, is to prescribe the limits of its own authority, and the States are bound to submit to the decision, and are not to be allowed to examine and decide for themselves when the barriers of the Constitution shall be overleaped, this is practically "a government without limitation of powers." The States are at once reduced to mere petty corporations, and the people are entirely at your mercy.

I have but one more word to add. In all the efforts that have been made by South Carolina to resist the unconstitutional laws which Congress has extended over them, she has kept steadily in view the preservation of the Union by the only means by which she believes it can be long preserved—a firm, manly, and steady resistance against usurpation. The measures of the federal government have, it is true, prostrated her interests, and will soon involve the whole South in irretrievable ruin. But even this evil, great as it is, is not the chief ground of our complaints. It is the principle involved in the contest—a principle which, substituting the discretion of Congress for the limitations of the Constitution, brings the States and the people to the feet of the federal government, and leaves them nothing they can call their own. Sir, if the measures of the federal government were less oppressive, we should still strive against this usurpation. The South is acting on a principle she has always held sacred—resistance to unauthorized taxation. These, sir, are the principles which induced the immortal Hampden to resist the payment of a tax of twenty shillings. Would twenty shillings have ruined his fortune? No! but the payment of half twenty shillings, on the principle on which it was demanded, would have made him a slave. Sir, if in acting on these high motives—if, animated by that ardent love of liberty which has always been the most prominent trait in the Southern character—we should be hurried beyond the bounds of a cold and calculating prudence, who is there, with one noble and generous sentiment in his bosom, that would not be disposed, in the language of Burke, to exclaim: "You must pardon something to the spirit of liberty!" [1]

- Used in his speech " On Conciliation with America."

WEBSTER

I

THE FIRST BUNKER HILL MONUMENT ORATION [1]

(1825)

Born in 1782, died in 1852; Member of Congress from New Hampshire in 1813–17, and from Massachusetts in 1823–27; United States Senator from Massachusetts in 1827–41; defeated for the Presidency in 1836; an unsuccessful candidate for the Whig nomination afterward; Secretary of State in 1841; negotiated the Ashburton Treaty in 1842; again elected Senator in 1845; made his " Seventh of March Speech " in 1850; Secretary of State in 1850; again unsuccessful for the Whig nomination for President in 1852.

THIS uncounted multitude before me and around me proves the feeling which the occasion has excited. These thousands of human faces, glowing with sympathy and joy, and from the impulses of a common gratitude turned reverently to heaven in this spacious temple of the firmament, proclaim that the day, the place, and the purpose of our assembling have made a deep impression on our hearts.

If, indeed, there be anything in local association fit to affect the mind of man, we need not strive to repress the emotions which agitate us

[1] Delivered at the laying of the corner-stone of the monument on June 17, 1825. Abridged.

here. We are among the sepulchers of our fathers. We are on ground distinguished by their valor, their constancy, and the shedding of their blood. We are here, not to fix an uncertain date in our annals, nor to draw into notice an obscure and unknown spot. If our humble purpose had never been conceived, if we ourselves had never been born, the 17th of June, 1775, would have been a day on which all subsequent history would have poured its light, and the eminence where we stand a point of attraction to the eyes of successive generations.

The Society whose organ I am was formed for the purpose of rearing some honorable and durable monument to the memory of the early friends of American Independence. They have thought that for this object no time could be more propitious than the present prosperous and peaceful period; that no place could claim preference over this memorable spot; and that no day could be more auspicious to the undertaking than the anniversary of the battle which was here fought. The foundation of that monument we have now laid. With solemnities suited to the occasion, with prayers to Almighty God for His blessing, and in the midst of this cloud of witnesses, we have begun the work. We trust it will be prosecuted, and that, springing from a broad foundation, rising high in massive solidity and unadorned grandeur, it may remain as long as heaven permits the works of man to last, a fit emblem, both of the events in memory of which it is raised, and of the gratitude of those who have reared it.

We know, indeed, that the record of illustrious actions is most safely deposited in the universal remembrance of mankind. We know, that if we could cause this structure to ascend, not only till it reached the skies, but till it pierced them, its broad surfaces could still contain but part of that which, in an age of knowledge, hath already been spread over the earth, and which history charges itself with making known to all future times. We know that no inscription on entablatures less broad than the earth itself can carry information of the events we commemorate where it has not already gone; and that no structure, which shall not outlive the duration of letters and knowledge among men, can prolong the memorial. But our object is, by this edifice, to show our own deep sense of the value and importance of the achievements of our ancestors; and by presenting this work of gratitude to the eye, to keep alive similar sentiments, and to foster a constant regard for the principles of the Revolution. Human beings are composed not of reason only, but of imagination also, and sentiment; and that is neither wasted nor misapplied which is appropriated to the purpose of giving right direction to sentiments, and opening proper springs of feeling in the heart.

We wish that, in those days of disaster, which,

as they come upon all nations, must be expected to come upon us also, desponding patriotism may turn its eyes hitherward, and be assured that the foundations of our national power are still strong. We wish that this column, rising toward heaven among the pointed spires of so many temples dedicated to God, may contribute also to produce, in all minds, a pious feeling of dependence and gratitude. We wish, finally, that the last object to the sight of him who leaves his native shore, and the first to gladden him who revisits it, may be something which shall remind him of the liberty and the glory of his country. Let it rise! let it rise, till it meet the sun in his coming; let the earliest light of the morning gild it, and parting day linger and play on its summit.

We still have among us some of those who were active agents in the scenes of 1775, and who are now here, from every quarter of New England, to visit once more, and under circumstances so affecting—I had almost said so overwhelming—this renowned theater of their courage and patriotism.

VENERABLE MEN! you have come down to us from a former generation.[1] Heaven has bounteously lengthened out your lives, that you might behold this joyous day. You are now where you stood fifty years ago, this very hour, with your brothers and your neighbors, shoulder to should-

---

[1] Some forty survivors of the Battle of Bunker Hill were present to hear this address.

27

er, in the strife for your country. Behold, how
altered! The same heavens are indeed over
your heads; the same ocean rolls at your feet;
but all else, how changed! You hear now no
roar of hostile cannon; you see no mixed volumes
of smoke and flame rising from burning Charlestown. The ground strewed with the dead and
the dying; the impetuous charge; the steady
and successful repulse; the loud call to repeated
assault; the summoning of all that is manly to repeated resistance; a thousand bosoms freely and
fearlessly bared in an instant to whatever of
terror there may be in war and death—all these
you have witnessed, but you witness them no
more.

All is peace. The heights of yonder metropolis, its towers and roofs, which you then saw
filled with wives and children and countrymen in distress and terror, and looking with un-
utterable emotions for the issue of the combat,
have presented you to-day with the sight of
its whole, happy population, come out to welcome and greet you with a universal jubilee.
Yonder proud ships, by a felicity of position
appropriately lying at the foot of this mount,
and seeming fondly to cling around it, are not
means of annoyance to you, but your country's
own means of distinction and defense. All is
peace; and God has granted you this sight of
your country's happiness, ere you slumber in
the grave. He has allowed you to behold and to
partake the reward of your patriotic toils; and

he has allowed us, your sons and countrymen, to meet you here, and in the name of the present generation, in the name of your country, in the name of liberty, to thank you!

But, alas! you are not all here! Time and the sword have thinned your ranks. Prescott, Putnam, Stark, Brooks, Reed, Pomeroy, Bridge!— our eyes seek for you in vain amid this broken band. You are gathered to your fathers, and live only to your country in her grateful remembrance and your own bright example. But let us not too much grieve that you have met the common fate of men. You lived at least long enough to know that your work had been nobly and successfully accomplished. You lived to see your country's independence established, and to sheathe your swords from war. On the light of Liberty you saw arise the light of Peace, like

> "Another morn,
> Risen on mid-noon"[1];

and the sky on which you closed your eyes was cloudless.

But, ah! Him![2] the first great martyr in

---

[1] These words are from the fifth book of Milton's "Paradise Lost," and occur in the remark made by Adam to Eve on discovering the approach of "The angelic Virtue," as follows:

> "Haste hither, Eve, and, worth thy sight, behold
> Eastward among these trees what glorious Shape
> Comes this way moving: Seems another morn
> Risen on mid-noon."

[2] Major-General Joseph Warren.

this great cause! Him! the premature victim of his own self-devoting heart! Him! the head of our civil councils, and the destined leader of our military bands, whom nothing brought hither but the unquenchable fire of his own spirit! Him! cut off by Providence in the hour of overwhelming anxiety and thick gloom; falling ere he saw the star of his country rise; pouring out his generous blood like water, before he knew whether it would fertilize a land of freedom or of bondage!—how shall I struggle with the emotions that stifle the utterance of thy name? Our poor work may perish; but thine shall endure! This monument may molder away; the solid ground it rests upon may sink down to a level with the sea; but thy memory shall not fail! Wheresoever among men a heart shall be found that beats to the transports of patriotism and liberty, its aspirations shall be to claim kindred with thy spirit.

But the scene amid which we stand does not permit us to confine our thoughts or our sympathies to those fearless spirits who hazarded or lost their lives on this consecrated spot. We have the happiness to rejoice here in the presence of a most worthy representation of the survivors of the whole Revolutionary army.

VETERANS! you are the remnant of many a well-fought field. You bring with you marks of honor from Trenton and Monmouth, from Yorktown, Camden, Bennington, and Saratoga. VETERANS OF HALF A CENTURY! when in your youthful days you put everything at hazard in your country's cause, good as that cause was, and sanguine as youth is, still your fondest hopes did not stretch onward to an hour like this! At a period to which you could not reasonably have expected to arrive, at a moment of national prosperity such as you could never have foreseen, you are now met here to enjoy the fellowship of old soldiers, and to receive the overflowings of a universal gratitude.

But your agitated countenances and your heaving breasts inform me that even this is not an unmixed joy. I perceive that a tumult of contending feelings rushes upon you. The images of the dead, as well as the persons of the living, present themselves before you. The scene overwhelms you, and I turn from it. May the Father of all mercies smile upon your declining years and bless them! And when you shall here have exchanged your embraces, when you shall once more have pressed the hands which have been so often extended to give succor in adversity, or grasped in the exultation of victory, then look abroad upon this lovely land which your young valor defended, and mark the happiness with which it is filled; yea, look abroad upon the whole earth, and see what a name you have contributed to give to your country, and what a praise you have added to freedom, and then rejoice in the sympathy and gratitude which beam upon your last days from the improved condition of mankind!

Information of these events, circulating throughout the world, at length reached the ears of one who now hears me.[1] He has not forgotten the emotion which the fame of Bunker Hill, and the name of Warren, excited in his youthful breast.

Sir, we are assembled to commemorate the establishment of great public principles of liberty and to do honor to the distinguished dead. The occasion is too severe for eulogy of the living. But, sir, your interesting relation to this country, the peculiar circumstances which surround you and surround us, call on me to express the happiness which we derive from your presence and aid in this solemn commemoration.

Fortunate, fortunate man! with what measure of devotion will you not thank God for the circumstances of your extraordinary life! You are connected with both hemispheres and with two generations. Heaven saw fit to ordain that the electric spark of liberty should be conducted, through you, from the New World to the Old; and we, who are now here to perform this duty of patriotism, have all of us long ago received it in charge from our fathers to cherish your name and your virtues. You will account it an instance of your good fortune, sir, that you crossed the seas to visit us at a time which enables you to be present at this solemnity. You now behold the field, the renown of which

[1] Lafayette, who sat among the Revolutionary officers, facing Webster as he spoke.

reached you in the heart of France, and caused a thrill in your ardent bosom. You see the lines of the little redoubt thrown up by the incredible diligence of Prescott; defended, to the last extremity, by his lion-hearted valor, and within which the corner-stone of our monument has now taken its position. You see where Warren fell, and where Parker, Gardner, McClary, Moore, and other early patriots fell with him. Those who survived that day, and whose lives have been prolonged to the present hour, are now around you. Some of them you have known in the trying scenes of the war. Behold! they now stretch forth their feeble arms to embrace you. Behold! they raise their trembling voices to invoke the blessing of God on you and yours for ever.

Sir, you have assisted us in laying the foundation of this structure. You have heard us rehearse, with our feeble commendation, the names of departed patriots. Monuments and eulogy belong to the dead. We give them this day to Warren and his associates. On other occasions they have been given to your more immediate companions in arms, to Washington, to Greene, to Gates, to Sullivan, and to Lincoln. W have become reluctant to grant these, our highest and last honors, further. We would gladly hold them yet back from the little remnant of that immortal band. *"Serus in cœlum redeas."* Illustrious as are your merits, yet far, oh, very far distant be the day, when any inscription shall bear your name, or any tongue pronounce its eulogy!

It is owing, perhaps, to this truth, that the interesting struggle of the Greeks has been suffered to go on so long, without a direct interference, either to wrest that country from its present masters, or to execute the system of pacification by force, and, with united strength, lay the neck of Christian and civilized Greek at the foot of the barbarian Turk. Let us thank God that we live in an age when something has influence besides the bayonet, and when the sternest authority does not venture to encounter the scorching power of public reproach. Any attempt of the kind I have mentioned should be met by one universal burst of indignation; the air of the civilized world ought to be made too warm to be comfortably breathed by any one who would hazard it.

It is, indeed, a touching reflection that, while in the fulness of our country's happiness we rear this monument to her honor, we look for instruction in our undertaking to a country which is now in fearful contest, not for works of art or memorials of glory, but for her own existence.[1] Let her be assured that she is not forgotten in the world; that her efforts are applauded, and that constant prayers ascend for her success. And let us cherish a confident hope for her final triumph. If the true spark of religious and civil liberty be kindled, it will

[1] Greece.

burn. Human agency can not extinguish it. Like the earth's central fire, it may be smothered for a time; the ocean may overwhelm it; mountains may press it down; but its inherent and unconquerable force will heave both the ocean and the land, and at some time or other, in some place or other, the volcano will break out and flame up to heaven.

And now, let us indulge an honest exultation in the conviction of the benefit which the example of our country has produced, and is likely to produce, on human freedom and human happiness. Let us endeavor to comprehend in all its magnitude, and to feel in all its importance, the part assigned to us in the great drama of human affairs. We are placed at the head of the system of representative and popular governments. Thus far our example shows that such governments are compatible, not only with respectability and power, but with repose, with peace, with security of personal rights, with good laws, and a just administration.

We are not propagandists. Wherever other systems are preferred, either as being thought better in themselves, or as better suited to existing conditions, we leave the preference to be enjoyed. Our history hitherto proves, however, that the popular form is practicable, and that with wisdom and knowledge men may govern themselves; and the duty incumbent on us is to preserve the consistency of this cheering example, and take care that nothing may weaken its authority with the world. If, in our case, the representative system ultimately fail, popular governments must be pronounced impossible. No combination of circumstances more favorable to the experiment can ever be expected to occur. The last hopes of mankind, therefore, rest with us; and if it should be proclaimed that our example had become an argument against the experiment, the knell of popular liberty would be sounded throughout the earth.

These are excitements to duty; but they are not suggestions of doubt. Our history and our condition, all that is gone before us, and all that surrounds us, authorize the belief, that popular governments, tho subject to occasional variations, in form perhaps not always for the better, may yet, in their general character, be as durable and permanent as other systems. We know, indeed, that in our country any other is impossible. The principle of free government adheres to the American soil. It is bedded in it, immovable as its mountains.

And let the sacred obligations which have devolved on this generation, and on us, sink deep into our hearts. Those who established our liberty and our government are daily dropping from among us. The great trust now descends to new hands. Let us apply ourselves to that which is presented to us, as our appropriate object. We can win no laurels in a war for independence. Earlier and worthier hands have gathered them all. Nor are there places for us by the side of Solon, and Alfred, and other founders of states. Our fathers have filled them. But there remains to us a great duty of defense and preservation; and there is opened to us, also, a noble pursuit, to which the spirit of the times strongly invites us. Our proper business is improvement. Let our age be the age of improvement. In a day of peace, let us advance the arts of peace and the works of peace. Let us develop the resources of our land, call forth its powers, build up its institutions, promote all its great interests, and see whether we also, in our day and generation, may not perform something worthy to be remembered. Let us cultivate a true spirit of union and harmony. In pursuing the great objects which our condition points out to us, let us act under a settled conviction, and an habitual feeling, that these twenty-four States are one country. Let our conceptions be enlarged to the circle of our duties. Let us extend our ideas over the whole of the vast field in which we are called to act. Let our object be, OUR COUNTRY, OUR WHOLE COUNTRY, AND NOTHING BUT OUR COUNTRY. And, by the blessing of God, may that country itself become a vast and splendid monument, not of oppression and terror, but of wisdom, of peace, and of liberty, upon which the world may gaze with admiration for ever!

II

IN REPLY TO HAYNE[1]

(1830)

WHEN the mariner has been tossed for many days in thick weather, and on an unknown sea, he naturally avails himself of the first pause in the storm, the earliest glance of the sun, to take his latitude and ascertain how far the elements have driven him from his true course. Let us imitate this prudence, and, before we float farther on the waves of this debate, refer to the point from which we departed, that we may at least be able to conjecture where we now are. I ask for the reading of the resolution before the Senate.

The gentleman, sir, in declining to postpone the debate, told the Senate, with the emphasis of his hand upon his heart, that there was something rankling *here,* which he wished to relieve. [Mr. Hayne rose and disclaimed having used the word *rankling.*] It would not, Mr. Presi-

[1] Delivered in the United States Senate on January 26, 1830, and sometimes called the speech on the Foote Resolution. For the text of this resolution, see note to Hayne's speech on a previous page. Webster had prepared no written copy of his speech, having with him at the time only some notes jotted down on a few sheets of paper. Its delivery, says Lodge, one of his biographers, "was practically extemporaneous." Webster, in reply to inquiries as to what he had done to prepare himself, is reported to have said that "his whole life had been a preparation for the reply to Hayne." Abridged.

dent, be safe for the honorable member to appeal to those around him, upon the question whether he did in fact make use of that word. But he may have been unconscious of it. At any rate, it is enough that he disclaims it. But still, with or without the use of that particular word, he had yet something *here,* he said, of which he wished to rid himself by an immediate reply. In this respect, sir, I have a great advantage over the honorable gentleman. There is nothing *here,* sir, which gives me the slightest uneasiness; neither fear, nor anger, nor that which is sometimes more troublesome than either, the consciousness of having been in the wrong.

Let me observe that the eulogium pronounced by the honorable gentleman on the character of the State of South Carolina, for her Revolutionary and other merits, meets my hearty concurrence. I shall not acknowledge that the honorable member goes before me in regard for whatever of distinguished talent, or distinguished character, South Carolina has produced. I claim part of the honor; I partake in the pride of her great names. I claim them for countrymen, one and all—the Laurenses, the Rutledges, the Pinckneys, the Sumters, the Marions—Americans all, whose fame is no more to be hemmed in by State lines, than their talents and patriotism were capable of being circumscribed within the same narrow limits. In their day and generation, they served and honored the country, and the whole country; and their

renown is of the treasures of the whole country.
Him whose honored name the gentleman himself bears,—does he esteem me less capable of
gratitude for his patriotism, or sympathy for his
sufferings, than if his eyes had first opened
upon the light of Massachusetts instead of South
Carolina? Sir, does he suppose it in his power
to exhibit a Carolina name so bright as to produce envy in my bosom? No, sir, increased gratification and delight, rather. I thank God that,
if I am gifted with little of the spirit which is
able to raise mortals to the skies, I have yet none,
as I trust, of that other spirit which would drag
angels down. When I shall be found, sir, in my
place here in the Senate, or elsewhere, to sneer
at public merit, because it happens to spring up
beyond the little limits of my own State or neighborhood; when I refuse, for any such cause or
for any cause, the homage due to American talent, to elevated patriotism, to sincere devotion to
liberty and the country; or, if I see an uncommon
endowment of heaven, if I see extraordinary
capacity and virtue, in any son of the South,
and if, moved by local prejudice or gangrened
by State jealousy, I get up here to abate the
tithe of a hair from his just character and just
fame, may my tongue cleave to the roof of my
mouth!

Sir, let me recur to pleasing recollections; let
me indulge in refreshing remembrance of the
past; let me remind you that, in early times,
no States cherished greater harmony, both of

principle and feeling, than Massachusetts and South Carolina. Would to God that harmony might again return! Shoulder to shoulder they went through the Revolution; hand in hand they stood round the administration of Washington, and felt his own great arm lean on them for support. Unkind feeling (if it exist), alienation, and distrust are the growth, unnatural to such soils, of false principles since sown. They are weeds, the seeds of which that same great arm never scattered.

Mr. President, I shall enter on no encomium upon Massachusetts; she needs none. There she is! Behold her, and judge for yourselves. There is her history; the world knows it by heart. The past, at least, is secure. There is Boston, and Concord, and Lexington, and Bunker Hill; and there they will remain for ever. The bones of her sons, falling in the great struggle for Independence, now lie mingled with the soil of every State from New England to Georgia; and there they will lie for ever. And, sir, where American Liberty raised its first voice, and where its youth was nurtured and sustained, there it still lives, in the strength of its manhood and full of its original spirit. If discord and disunion shall wound it, if party strife and blind ambition shall hawk at and tear it, if folly and madness, if uneasiness under salutary and necessary restraint, shall succeed in separating it from that Union by which alone its existence is made sure, it will stand, in the end, by the side of that cradle in which its infancy was rocked; it will stretch forth its arm with whatever of vigor it may still retain over the friends who gather round it; and it will fall at last, if fall it must, amid the proudest monuments of its own glory, and on the very spot of its origin.

There yet remains to be performed, Mr. President, by far the most grave and important duty which I feel to be devolved on me by this occasion. It is to state, and to defend, what I conceive to be the true principles of the Constitution under which we are here assembled. I might well have desired that so weighty a task should have fallen into other and abler hands. I could have wished that it should have been executed by those whose character and experience give weight and influence to their opinions, such as can not possibly belong to mine. But, sir, I have met the occasion, not sought it; and I shall proceed to state my own sentiments, without challenging for them any particular regard, with studied plainness, and as much precision as possible.

I understand the honorable gentleman from South Carolina to maintain that it is a right of the State Legislatures to interfere whenever, in their judgment, this government transcends its constitutional limits, and to arrest the operation of its laws.

I understand him to maintain this right, as a right existing *under* the Constitution, not as a right to overthrow it on the ground of extreme necessity, such as would justify violent revolution.

I understand him to maintain an authority, on the part of the States, thus to interfere, for the purpose of correcting the exercise of power by the general government, of checking it, and of compelling it to conform to their opinion of the extent of its powers. I understand him to maintain that the ultimate power of judging of the constitutional extent of its own authority is not lodged exclusively in the general government, or any branch of it; but that, on the contrary, the States may lawfully decide for themselves, and each State for itself, whether, in a given case, the act of the general government transcends its power.

I understand him to insist that, if the exigency of the case, in the opinion of any State government, require it, such State government may, by its own sovereign authority, annul an act of the general government which it deems plainly and palpably unconstitutional.

This is the sum of what I understand from him to be the South Carolina doctrine, and the doctrine which he maintains. I propose to consider it, and compare it with the Constitution. Allow me to say, as a preliminary remark, that I call this the South Carolina doctrine only because the gentleman himself has so denominated it. I do not feel at liberty to say that South Carolina, as a State, has ever advanced these sentiments. I hope she has not, and never may. That a great majority of her people are opposed to the tariff laws is doubtless true. That a majority, somewhat less than that just mentioned, conscientiously believe these laws unconstitutional may probably also be true. But that any majority holds to the right of direct State interference at State discretion, the right of nullifying acts of Congress by acts of State legislation, is more than I know, and what I shall be slow to believe.

That there are individuals besides the honorable gentlemen who do maintain these opinions, is quite certain. I recollect the recent expression of a sentiment, which circumstances attending its utterance and publication justify us in supposing was not unpremeditated. "The sovereignty of the State,—never to be controlled, construed, or decided on, but by her own feelings of honorable justice."

We all know that civil institutions are established for the public benefit, and that when they cease to answer the ends of their existence they may be changed. But I do not understand the doctrine now contended for to be that which, for the sake of distinction, we may call the right of revolution. I understand the gentleman to maintain that it is constitutional to interrupt the administration of the Constitution itself, in the hands of those who are chosen and sworn to administer it, by the direct interference, in form of law, of the States, in virtue of their sovereign capacity. The inherent right in the people to reform their government I do not deny; and they have another right, and that is to resist unconstitutional laws, without overturning the government. It is no doctrine of mine that unconstitutional laws bind the people. The great question is, Whose prerogative is it to decide on the constitutionality or unconstitutionality of the laws? On that the main debate hinges.

The proposition that in case of a supposed violation of the Constitution by Congress the States have a constitutional right to interfere and annul the law of Congress, is the proposition of the gentleman. I do not admit it. If the gentleman had intended no more than to assert the right of revolution for justifiable cause, he would have said only what all agree to. But I can not conceive that there can be a middle course, between submission to the laws when regularly pronounced constitutional, on the one hand, and open resistance (which is revolution or rebellion) on the other.

This leads us to inquire into the origin of this government and the source of its power. Whose agent is it? Is it the creature of the State Legislatures, or the creature of the people? If the government of the United States be the agent of the State governments, then they may control it, provided they can agree in the manner of controlling it; if it be the agent of the people, then the people alone can control it, restrain it, modify, or reform it. It is observable enough that the doctrine for which the honorable gentleman contends leads him to the necessity of maintaining, not only that this general government is the creature of the States, but that it is the creature of each of the States severally, so that each may assert the power for itself of determining whether it acts within the limits of its authority. It is the servant of four-and-twenty masters, of different wills and different purposes, and yet bound to obey all. This absurdity (for it seems no less) arises from a misconception as to the origin of this government and its true character. It is, sir, the people's Constitution, the people's government, made for the people, made by the people, and answerable to the people. The people of the United States have declared that this Constitution shall be the supreme law. We must either admit the proposition or dispute their authority.

The States are, unquestionably, sovereign, so far as their sovereignty is not affected by the supreme law. But the State Legislatures, as political bodies, however sovereign, are yet not sovereign over the people. So far as the people have given power to the general government, so far the grant is unquestionably good, and the government holds of the people, and not of the State governments. We are all agents of the same supreme power, the people. The general government and the State governments derive their authority from the same source. Neither can, in relation to the other, be called primary, tho one is definite and restricted, and the other general and residuary. The national government possesses those powers which it can be shown the people have conferred on it, and no more. All the rest belongs to the State governments, or to the people themselves. So far as the people have restrained State sovereignty, by the expression of their will, in the Constitution of the United States, so far, it must be admitted, State sovereignty is effectually controlled. I do not contend that it is, or ought to be, controlled farther.

The sentiment to which I have referred propounds that State sovereignty is only to be controlled by its own "feeling of justice"; that is to say, it is not to be controlled at all, for one who is to follow his own feelings is under no legal control. Now, however men may think this ought to be, the fact is, that the people of the United States have chosen to impose control on State sovereignties. There are those, doubtless, who wish they had been left without restraint; but the Constitution has ordered the matter differently. To make war, for instance, is an exercise of sovereignty; but the Constitution declares that no State shall make war. To coin money is another exercise of sovereign power; but no State is at liberty to coin money. Again, the Constitution says that no sovereign State shall be so sovereign as to make a treaty. These prohibitions, it must be confessed, are a control on the State sovereignty of South Carolina, as well as of the other States, which does not arise "from her own feelings of honorable justice." The opinion referred to, therefore, is in defiance of the plainest provisions of the Constitution.

In Carolina, the tariff is a palpable, deliberate usurpation; Carolina, therefore, may nullify it, and refuse to pay the duties. In Pennsylvania it is both clearly constitutional and highly expedient; and there the duties are to be paid. And yet we live under a government of uniform laws, and under a Constitution, too, which contains an express provision, as it happens, that all duties shall be equal in all the States. Does not this approach absurdity?

If there be no power to settle such questions, independent of either of the States, is not the whole Union a rope of sand? Are we not thrown back again, precisely upon the old Confederation?

It is too plain to be argued. Four-and-twenty interpreters of constitutional law, each with a power to decide for itself, and none with authority to bind anybody else, and this constitutional law the only bond of their union! What is such a state of things but a mere connection during pleasure, or, to use the phraseology of the times, *during feeling?* And that feeling, too, not the feeling of the people who established the Constitution, but the feeling of the State governments.

Resolutions, sir, have been recently passed by the Legislature of South Carolina. I need not refer to them; they go no farther than the honorable gentleman himself has gone, and I hope not so far. I content myself, therefore, with debating the matter with him.

And now, sir, what I have first to say on this subject is, that at no time, and under no circumstances, has New England, or any State in New England, or any respectable body of persons in New England, or any public man of standing in New England, put forth such a doctrine as this Carolina doctrine.

The gentleman has found no case, he can find none, to support his own opinions by New England authority. New England has studied the Constitution in other schools and under other teachers. She looks upon it with other regards, and deems more highly and reverently both of its just authority and its utility and excellence. The history of her legislative proceedings may be traced. The ephemeral effusions of temporary bodies, called together by the excitement of the occasion, may be hunted up; they have been hunted up. The opinions and votes of her public men, in and out of Congress, may be explored; it will all be in vain. The Carolina doctrine can derive from her neither countenance nor support. She rejects it now; she always did reject it; and till she loses her senses, she always will reject it.

The honorable member has referred to expressions on the subject of the embargo law, made in this place, by an honorable and venerable gentleman, now favoring us with his presence. He quotes that distinguished senator as saying that, in his judgment, the embargo law was unconstitutional, and that therefore, in his opinion, the people were not bound to obey it. That, sir, is perfectly constitutional language. An unconstitutional law is not binding; *but then it does not rest with a resolution or a law of a State Legislature to decide whether an act of Congress be or be not constitutional.* An unconstitutional act of Congress would not bind the people of this District, altho they have no Legislature to interfere in their behalf; and, on the other hand, a constitutional law of Congress does bind the citizen of every State, aitho all their Legislatures should undertake to annul it by act or resolution. The venerable Connecticut senator is a constitutional lawyer of sound principles and enlarged knowledge, a statesman practised and experienced, bred in the company of Washington, and holding just views upon the nature of our governments. He believes the embargo unconstitutional, and so did others; but what then? Who did he suppose was to decide that question? The State Legislatures? Certainly not. No such sentiment ever escaped his lips.

Let us follow up, sir, this New England opposition to the embargo laws; let us trace it till we discern the principle which controlled and governed New England throughout the whole course of that opposition. We shall then see what similarity there is between the New England school of constitutional opinions, and this modern Carolina school. The gentleman, I think, read a petition from some single individual addressed to the Legislature of Massachusetts, asserting the Carolina doctrine; that is, the right of State interference to arrest the laws of the Union. The fate of that petition shows the sentiment of the Legislature. It met no favor. The opinions of Massachusetts were very different. They had been expressed in 1798, in answer to the resolutions of Virginia, and she did not depart from them, nor bend them to the times. Misgoverned, wronged, oppressed, as she felt herself to be, she still held fast her integrity to the Union. The gentleman may find in her proceedings much evidence of dissatisfaction with the measures of government, and great and deep dislike to the embargo—all this makes the case so much the stronger for her; for, notwithstanding all this dissatisfaction and dislike, she still claimed no right to sever the bonds of the Union. There was heat and there was anger in her political feeling.

Be it so; but neither her heat nor her anger betrayed her into infidelity to the government. The gentleman labors to prove that she disliked the embargo as much as South Carolina dislikes the tariff, and expressed her dislike as strongly. Be it so; but did she propose the Carolina remedy? Did she threaten to interfere, by State authority, to annul the laws of the Union? That is the question for the gentleman's consideration.

No doubt, sir, a great majority of the people of New England conscientiously believed the embargo law of 1807 unconstitutional; as conscientiously, certainly, as the people of South Carolina hold that opinion of the tariff. They reasoned thus: Congress has power to regulate commerce; but here is a law, they said, stopping all commerce, and stopping it indefinitely. The law is perpetual; that is, it is not limited in point of time, and must of course continue until it shall be repealed by some other law. It is perpetual, therefore, as the law against treason or murder. Now, is this regulating commerce or destroying it? Is it guiding, controlling, giving the rule to commerce, as a subsisting thing, or is it putting an end to it altogether? Nothing is more certain than that a majority in New England deemed this law a violation of the Constitution. The very case required by the gentleman to justify State interference had then arisen. Massachusetts believed this law to be "a deliberate, palpable, and dangerous exercise of a power not granted by the Constitution." Deliberate it was, for it was long continued; palpable she thought it, as no words in the Constitution gave the power, and only a construction, in her opinion most violent, raised it; dangerous it was, since it threatened utter ruin to her most important interests.

Here, then, was a Carolina case. How did Massachusetts deal with it? It was, as she thought, a plain, manifest, palpable violation of

the Constitution, and it brought ruin to her doors.
Thousands of families, and hundreds of thousands of individuals, were beggared by it. While
she saw and felt all this, she saw and felt also
that, as a measure of national policy, it was perfectly futile; that the country was in no way
benefited by that which caused so much individual distress; that it was efficient only for the production of evil, and all that evil inflicted on
ourselves. In such a case, under such circumstances, how did Massachusetts demean herself?
Sir, she remonstrated, she memorialized, she addressed herself to the general government, not
exactly "with the concentrated energy of
passion," but with her own strong sense, and
the energy of sober conviction.

But she did not interpose the arm of her own
power to arrest the law and break the embargo.
Far from it. Her principles bound her to two
things, and she followed her principles, lead
where they might: first, to submit to every constitutional law of Congress; and secondly, if
the constitutional validity of the law be doubted,
to refer that question to the decision of the proper tribunals. The first principle is vain and ineffectual without the second. A majority of us
in New England believed the embargo law unconstitutional; but the great question was, and
always will be in such cases, Who is to decide
this? Who is to judge between the people and
the government? And, sir, it is quite plain that
the Constitution of the United States confers

on the government itself, to be exercised by its appropriate department, and under its own responsibility to the people, this power of deciding ultimately and conclusively upon the just extent of its own authority. If this had not been done, we should not have advanced a single step beyond the old Confederation.

Being fully of the opinion that the embargo law was unconstitutional, the people of New England were yet equally clear in the opinion (it was a matter they did not doubt upon) that the question, after all, must be decided by the judicial tribunals of the United States. Before these tribunals, therefore, they brought the question. Under the provisions of the law, they had given bonds to millions in amount, and which were alleged to be forfeited. They suffered the bonds to be sued, and thus raised the question. In the old-fashioned way of settling disputes, they went to law. The case came to hearing and solemn argument; and he who espoused their cause, and stood up for them against the validity of the embargo act, was none other than the great man of whom the gentleman has made honorable mention, Samuel Dexter.[1]

He was then, sir, in the fulness of his knowledge and the maturity of his strength. He had retired from long and distinguished public service here,

[1] Senator from Massachusetts, 1799–1800; secretary of war, 1800; secretary of the Treasury, 1800–1804; candidate in 1816 for governor of Massachusetts, on a platform opposing the Hartford Convention. Defeated by 2,000 votes.

to the renewed pursuit of professional duties, carrying with him all that enlargement and expansion, all the new strength and force, which an acquaintance with the more general subjects discussed in the national councils is capable of adding to professional attainment, in a mind of true greatness and comprehension. He was a lawyer, and he was also a statesman. He had studied the Constitution, when he filled public station, that he might defend it; he had examined its principles that he might maintain them. More than all men, or at least as much as any man, he was attached to the general government and to the union of the States. His feelings and opinions all ran in that direction. A question of constitutional law, too, was, of all subjects, that one which was best suited to his talents and learning. Aloof from technicality, and unfettered by artificial rule, such a question gave opportunity for that deep and clear analysis, that mighty grasp of principle, which so much distinguished his higher efforts. His very statement was argument; his inference seemed demonstration. The earnestness of his own conviction wrought conviction in others. One was convinced, and believed, and assented, because it was gratifying, delightful, to think, and feel, and believe, in unison with an intellect of such evident superiority.

Sir, the human mind is so constituted that the merits of both sides of a controversy appear very clear and very palpable to those who respectively espouse them; and both sides usually grow clearer as the controversy advances. South Carolina sees unconstitutionality in the tariff; she sees oppression there also, and she sees danger. Pennsylvania, with a vision not less sharp, looks at the same tariff, and sees no such thing in it; she sees it all constitutional, all useful, all safe. The faith of South Carolina is strengthened by opposition, and she now not only sees, but *resolves,* that the tariff is palpably unconstitutional, oppressive, and dangerous; but Pennsylvania, not to be behind her neighbors, and equally willing to strengthen her own faith by a confident asseveration, *resolves,* also, and gives to every warm affirmative of South Carolina, a plain, downright, Pennsylvania negative. South Carolina, to show the strength and unity of her opinion, brings her assembly to a unanimity, within seven voices; Pennsylvania, not to be outdone in this respect any more than in others, reduces her dissentient fraction to a single vote.

Now, sir, again I ask the gentleman, What is to be done? Are these States both right? Is he bound to consider them both right? If not, which is in the wrong? or rather, which has the best right to decide? And if he, and if I, are not to know what the Constitution means, and what it is, till those two State legislatures, and the twenty-two others, shall agree in its construction, what have we sworn to when we have sworn to maintain it? I was forcibly struck, sir, with one reflection, as the gentleman went on in his speech. He quoted Mr. Madison's resolutions, to prove that a State may interfere, in a case of deliberate, palpable, and dangerous exercise of a power not granted. The honorable member supposes the tariff law to be such an exercise of power; and that consequently a case has arisen in which the State may, if it see fit, interfere by its own law. Now it so happens, nevertheless, that Mr. Madison deems this same tariff law quite constitutional. Instead of a clear and palpable violation, it is, in his judgment, no violation at all. So that, while they use his authority for a hypothetical case, they reject it in the very case before them. All this, sir, shows the inherent futility—I had almost used a stronger word—of conceding this power of interference to the State, and then attempting to secure it from abuse by imposing qualifications of which the States themselves are to judge. One of two things is true: either the laws of the Union are beyond the discretion and beyond the control of the States; or else we have no constitution of general government, and are thrust back again to the days of the Confederation.

Let me here say, sir, that if the gentleman's doctrine had been received and acted upon in New England, in the times of the embargo and nonintercourse, we should probably not now have been here. The government would very likely have gone to pieces and crumbled into dust.

No stronger case can ever arise than existed under those laws; no States can ever entertain a clearer conviction than the New England States then entertained; and if they had been under the influence of that heresy of opinion, as I must call it, which the honorable member espouses, this Union would, in all probability, have been scattered to the four winds. I ask the gentleman, therefore, to apply his principles to that case; I ask him to come forth and declare whether, in his opinion, the New England States would have been justified in interfering to break up the embargo system under the conscientious opinions which they held upon it? Had they a right to annul that law? Does he admit or deny? If what is thought palpably unconstitutional in South Carolina justifies that State in arresting the progress of the law, tell me whether that which was thought palpably unconstitutional also in Massachusetts would have justified her in doing the same thing? Sir, I deny the whole doctrine. It has not a foot of ground in the Constitution to stand on. No public man of reputation ever advanced it in Massachusetts in the warmest times, or could maintain himself upon it there at any time.

I must now beg to ask, sir, Whence is this supposed right of the States derived? Where do they find the power to interfere with the laws of the Union? Sir, the opinion which the honorable gentleman maintains is a notion founded on a total misapprehension, in my judgment, of the origin of this government, and of the foundation on which it stands. I hold it to be a popular government, erected by the people; those who administer it responsible to the people; and itself capable of being amended and modified, just as the people may choose it should be. It is as popular, just as truly emanating from the people, as the State governments. It is created for one purpose; the State governments for another. It has its own powers; they have theirs. There is no more authority with them to arrest the operation of a law of Congress, than with Congress to arrest the operation of their laws.

We are here to administer a Constitution emanating immediately from the people, and trusted by them to our administration. It is not the creature of the State governments. It is of no moment to the argument, that certain acts of the State Legislatures are necessary to fill our seats in this body. That is not one of their original State powers, a part of the sovereignty of the State. It is a duty which the people, by the Constitution itself, have imposed on the State Legislatures, and which they might have left to be performed elsewhere, if they had seen fit. So they have left the choice of president with electors; but all this does not affect the proposition that this whole government, president, Senate, and House of Representatives, is a popular government. It leaves it still all its popular character. The governor of a State (in some of the States) is chosen, not directly by the people, but by those who are chosen by the people, for the purpose of performing, among other duties, that of electing a governor. Is the government of the State, on that account, not a popular government? This government, sir, is the independent offspring of the popular will. It is not the creature of State Legislatures; nay, more, if the whole truth must be told, the people brought it into existence, established it, and have hitherto supported it, for the very purpose, among others, of imposing certain salutary restraints on State sovereignties. The States can not now make war; they can not contract alliances; they can not make, each for itself, separate regulations of commerce; they can not lay imposts; they can not coin money. If this Constitution, sir, be the creature of State Legislatures, it must be admitted that it has obtained a strange control over the volitions of its creators.

To avoid all possibility of being misunderstood, allow me to repeat again, in the fullest manner, that I claim no powers for the government by forced or unfair construction. I admit that it is a government of strictly limited powers—of enumerated, specified, and particularized powers, and that whatsoever is not granted is withheld. But notwithstanding all this, and however the grant of powers may be expressed, its limit and extent may yet, in some cases, admit of doubt; and the general government would be good for nothing, it would be incapable of long existing, if some mode had not been provided in which those doubts, as they should arise, might be peaceably, but authoritatively, solved.

Mr. President, I have thus stated the reasons of my dissent to the doctrines which have been advanced and maintained. I am conscious of having detained you and the Senate much too long. I was drawn into the debate with no previous deliberation, such as is suited to the discussion of so grave and important a subject. But it is a subject of which my heart is full, and I have not been willing to suppress the utterance of its spontaneous sentiments. I can not, even now, persuade myself to relinquish it, without expressing once more my deep conviction that, since it respects nothing less than the Union of the States, it is of most vital and essential importance to the public happiness.

I profess, sir, in my career hitherto, to have kept steadily in view the prosperity and honor of the whole country, and the preservation of our federal Union. It is to that Union we owe our safety at home, and our consideration and dignity abroad. It is to that Union that we are chiefly indebted for whatever makes us most proud of our country. That Union we reached only by the discipline of our virtues in the severe school of adversity. It had its origin in the necessities of disordered finance, prostrate commerce, and ruined credit. Under its benign influences, these great interests immediately awoke, as from the dead, and sprang forth with newness of life. Every year of its duration has teemed with fresh proofs of its utility and its blessings; and altho our territory has stretched out wider and wider, and our population spread farther and farther, they have not outrun its protection or its benefits. It has been to us all a copious fountain of national, social, and personal happiness.

I have not allowed myself, sir, to look beyond the Union, to see what might lie hidden in the dark recess behind. I have not coolly weighed the chances of preserving liberty when the bonds that unite us together shall be broken asunder. I have not accustomed myself to hang over the precipice of disunion, to see whether, with my short sight, I can fathom the depth of the abyss below; nor could I regard him as a safe counselor in the affairs of this government, whose thoughts should be mainly bent on considering, not how the Union may be best preserved, but how tolerable might be the condition of the people when it should be broken up and destroyed.

While the Union lasts, we have high, exciting, gratifying prospects spread out before us, for us and our children. Beyond that I seek not to penetrate the veil. God grant that, in my day, at least, that curtain may not rise! God grant that on my vision never may be opened what lies behind! When my eyes shall be turned to behold for the last time the sun in heaven, may I not see him shining on the broken and dishonored fragments of a once glorious Union; on States dissevered, discordant, belligerent; on a land rent with civil feuds, or drenched, it may be, in fraternal blood! Let their last feeble and lingering glance rather behold the gorgeous ensign of the Republic, now known and honored throughout the earth, still full high advanced, its arms and trophies streaming in their original luster, not a stripe erased or polluted, nor a single star obscured, bearing for its motto no such miserable interrogatory as, "What is all this worth?" nor those other words of delusion and folly, "Liberty first and Union afterward"; but everywhere, spread all over in characters of living light, blazing on all its ample folds, as they float over the sea and over the land, and in every wind under the whole heavens, that other sentiment, dear to every true American heart—Liberty *and* Union, now and for ever, one and inseparable!

III

ON THE CLAY COMPROMISE[1]

(1850)

SLAVERY did exist in the States before the adoption of this Constitution, and at that time. Let us, therefore, consider for a moment what was the state of sentiment, North and South, in regard to slavery—in regard to slavery, at the time this Constitution was adopted. A remarkable change has taken place since; but what did the wise and great men of all parts of the country think of slavery then? In what estima-

[1] Otherwise known as "The Seventh of March Speech." Delivered in the United States Senate in support of Clay's compromise resolutions. Abridged. Curtis, the biographer of Webster, admits that this speech met with general disfavor throughout the North. Schurz describes the antislavery men as contemplating "the fall of an archangel." Webster was called "a recreant son of Massachusetts," "a fallen star," and "a bankrupt politician gambling for the presidency," while Whittier in one of his poems wrote:

> "All else is gone; from those great eyes
>   The soul has fled;
> When faith is lost, when honor dies,
>   The man is dead.

> "Then pay the reverence of old days
>   To his dead fame;
> Walk backward with averted gaze
>   And hide his shame."

The calmer judgment of later times has dealt more favorably with Webster's speech. It has even been held that owing to its

tion did they hold it at the time when this Constitution was adopted? It will be found, sir, if we will carry ourselves by historical research back to that day, and ascertain men's opinions by authentic records still existing among us, that there was no diversity of opinion between the North and the South upon the subject of slavery. It will be found that both parts of the country held it equally an evil, a moral and political evil. It will not be found that, either at the North or at the South, there was much, tho there was some, invective against slavery as inhuman and cruel.

The great ground of objection to it was political; that it weakened the social fabric; that, taking the place of free labor, society became less strong and labor less productive; and therefore we find from all the eminent men of the time the clearest expression of their opinion that slavery is an evil. They ascribed its existence here, not without truth, and not without some acerbity of temper and force of language, to the injurious policy of the mother country, who, to favor the navigator, had entailed these evils upon the Colonies.

The whole interest of the South became con-

influence the war was postponed for ten years, the North thus gaining time to increase its resources. Blaine has pointed out that in 1861 a recession from the antislavery position of an earlier period had become with Republicans "part of the conciliatory policy of the hour," and that they, as led by Seward, "took precisely the same ground held by Mr. Webster in 1850, and acted from precisely the same motives that inspired 'The Seventh of March Speech.'"

nected, more or less, with the extension of slavery. If we look back to the history of the commerce of this country in the early years of this government, what were our exports? Cotton was hardly, or but to a very limited extent, known. In 1791 the first parcel of cotton of the growth of the United States was exported, and amounted only to 19,200 pounds. It has gone on increasing rapidly, until the whole crop may now, perhaps, in a season of great product and high prices, amount to a hundred millions of dollars. In the years I have mentioned, there was more of wax, more of indigo, more of rice, more of almost every article of export from the South, than of cotton. When Mr. Jay negotiated the treaty of 1794 with England, it is evident from the Twelfth Article of the Treaty, which was suspended by the Senate, that he did not know that cotton was exported at all from the United States.

Mr. President, in the excited times in which we live, there is found to exist a state of crimination and recrimination between the North and South. There are lists of grievances produced by each; and those grievances, real or supposed, alienate the minds of one portion of the country from the other, exasperate the feelings, and subdue the sense of fraternal affection, patriotic love, and mutual regard. I shall bestow a little attention, sir, upon these various grievances existing on the one side and on the other. I begin with complaints of the South. I will not answer, further than I have, the general statements of the honorable senator from South Carolina, that the North has prospered at the expense of the South in consequence of the manner of administering this government, in the collection of its revenues, and so forth. These are disputed topics, and I have no inclination to enter into them.

But I will allude to other complaints of the South, and especially to one which has, in my opinion, just foundation; and that is, that there has been found at the North, among individuals and among legislators, a disinclination to perform fully their constitutional duties in regard to the return of persons bound to service who have escaped into the free States. In that respect, the South, in my judgment, is right, and the North is wrong. Every member of every Northern Legislature is bound by oath, like every other officer in the country, to support the Constitution of the United States; and the article of the Constitution which says to these States that they shall deliver up fugitives from service, is as binding in honor and conscience as any other article. No man fulfils his duty in any Legislature who sets himself to find excuses, evasions, escapes from this constitutional obligation. I have always thought that the Constitution addressed itself to the Legislatures of the States or to the States themselves. It says that those persons escaping to other States "shall be delivered up," and I confess I have always been of the opinion that it was an injunction upon the States themselves. When it is said that a person escaping into another State, and coming therefore within the jurisdiction of that State, shall be delivered up, it seems to me the import of the clause is, that the State itself, in obedience to the Constitution, shall cause him to be delivered up. That is my judgment. I have always entertained that opinion, and I entertain it now.

Then, sir, there are the abolition societies, of which I am unwilling to speak, but in regard to which I have very clear notions and opinions. I do not think them useful. I think their operations for the last twenty years have produced nothing good or valuable. At the same time, I believe thousands of their members to be honest and good men, perfectly well-meaning men. They have excited feelings; they think they must do something for the cause of liberty; and, in their sphere of action, they do not see what else they can do than to contribute to an abolition press, or an abolition society, or to pay an abolition lecturer.

I do not mean to impute gross motives even to the leaders of these societies, but I am not blind to the consequences of their proceedings. I can not but see what mischief their interference with the South has produced. And is it not plain to every man? Let any gentleman who entertains doubts on this point, recur to the debates in the Virginia House of Delegates in 1832, and he will see with what freedom a proposition made by Mr. Jefferson Randolph, for the gradual abolition of slavery was discussed in that body. Every one spoke of slavery as he thought; very ignominious and disparaging names and epithets were applied to it. The debates in the House of Delegates on that occasion, I believe were all published. They were read by every colored man who could read, and to those who could not read, those debates were read by others. At that time Virginia was not unwilling or afraid to discuss this question, and to let that part of her population know as much of the discussion as they could learn.

That was in 1832. As has been said by the honorable member from South Carolina, these abolition societies commenced their course of action in 1835. It is said, I do not know how true it may be, that they sent incendiary publications into the slave States; at any rate, they attempted to arouse, and did arouse, a very strong feeling; in other words, they created great agitation in the North against Southern slavery. Well, what was the result? The bonds of the slaves were bound more firmly than before; their rivets were more strongly fastened. Public opinion, which in Virginia had begun to be exhibited against slavery, and was opening out for the discussion of the question, drew back and shut itself up in its castle. I wish to know whether anybody in Virginia can now talk openly, as Mr. Randolph, Governor McDowel, and others talked in 1832, and sent their remarks to the Press? We all know the fact, and we all know the cause; and everything that these agitating people have done has been, not to enlarge, but to restrain, not to set free, but to bind faster, the slave population of the South.

Mr. President, I should much prefer to have heard from every member on this floor declarations of opinion that this Union could never be dissolved, than the declaration of opinion by anybody, that in any case, under the pressure of any circumstances, such a dissolution was possible. I hear with distress and anguish the word "secession," especially when it falls from the lips of those who are patriotic, and known to the country, and known all over the world for their political services. Secession! Peaceable secession! Sir, your eyes and mine are never destined to see that miracle. The dismemberment of this vast country without convulsion! The breaking up of the fountains of the great deep without ruffling the surface! Who is so foolish—I beg everybody's pardon—as to expect to see any such thing?

Sir, he who sees these States now revolving in harmony around a common center, and expects to see them quit their places and fly off without convulsion, may look the next hour to see the heavenly bodies rush from their spheres, and jostle against each other in the realms of space, without causing the crush of the universe. There can be no such thing as a peaceable secession. Peaceable secession is an utter impossibility. Is the great Constitution under which we live, covering this whole country, is it to be thawed and melted away by secession, as the snows on the mountain melt under the influence of a vernal sun, disappear almost unobserved, and run off? No, sir! No, sir! I will not state what might produce the disruption of the Union; but, sir, I see, as plainly as I see the sun in heaven, what the disruption itself must produce; I see that it must produce war, and such a war as I will not describe, *in its twofold character.*

Peaceable secession!—peaceable secession! The concurrent agreement of all the members of this great Republic to separate! A voluntary separation, with alimony on one side and on the other. Why, what would be the result? Where is the line to be drawn? What States are to secede? What is to remain American? What am I to be? An American no longer? Am I to become a sectional man, a local man, a separatist, with no country in common with the gentlemen who sit around me here, or who fill the other House of Congress? Heaven forbid! Where is the flag of the Republic to remain? Where is the eagle still to tower?—or is he to cower, and shrink, and fall to the ground?

Why, sir, our ancestors—our fathers and our grandfathers, those of them that are yet living among us, with prolonged lives—would rebuke and reproach us; and our children and our grandchildren would cry out shame upon us, if we, of this generation, should dishonor these ensigns of the power of the government and the harmony of that Union, which is every day felt among us with so much joy and gratitude. What is to become of the army? What is to become of the navy? What is to become of the public lands? How is any one of the thirty States to defend itself?

Sir, we could not sit down here to-day, and draw a line of separation that would satisfy any five men in the country. There are natural causes that would keep and tie us together; and there are social and domestic relations which we could not break if we would, and which we should not if we could.

Sir, nobody can look over the face of this country at the present moment, nobody can see where its population is the most dense and growing, without being ready to admit, and compelled to admit, that ere long the strength of America will be in the valley of the Mississippi. Well, now, sir, I beg to inquire what the wildest enthusiast has to say on the possibility of cutting that river in two, and leaving free States at its source and on its branches, and slave States down near its mouth, each forming a separate government? Pray, sir, let me say to the people of this country, that these things are worthy of their pondering and of their consideration. Here, sir, are five millions of freemen in the free States north of the river Ohio.

Can anybody suppose that this population can be severed, by a line that divides them from the territory of a foreign and alien government, down somewhere, the Lord knows where, upon the lower banks of the Mississippi? What would become of Missouri? Will she join the *arrondissement* of the slave States? Shall the man from the Yellowstone and the Platte be connected, in the new Republic, with the man who lives on the southern extremity of the Cape of Florida? Sir, I am ashamed to pursue this line of remark. I dislike it; I have an utter disgust for it. I would rather hear of natural blasts and mildews, war, pestilence, and famine, than to hear gentlemen talk of secession. To break up this great government! to dismember this glorious country! to astonish Europe with an act of folly such as Europe for two centuries has never beheld in any government or any people! No, sir! no, sir! There will be no secession! Gentlemen are not serious when they talk of secession.

And now, Mr. President, instead of speaking of the possibility or utility of secession, instead of dwelling in these caverns of darkness, instead of groping with those ideas so full of all that is horrid and horrible, let us come out into the light of day; let us enjoy the fresh air of liberty and union; let us cherish those hopes which belong to us; let us devote ourselves to those great objects that are fit for our consideration and our action; let us raise our conceptions to the magnitude and the importance of the duties that devolve upon us; let our comprehension be as broad as the country for which we act, our aspirations as high as its certain destiny; let us not be pigmies in a case that calls for men. Never did there devolve on any generation of men higher trusts than now devolve upon us, for the preservation of this Constitution, and the harmony and peace of all who are destined to live under it. Let us make our generation one of the strongest and brightest links in that golden chain, which is destined, I fondly believe, to grapple the people of all the States to this Constitution for ages to come.

We have a great, popular, constitutional government, guarded by law and by judicature, and defended by the whole affections of the people. No monarchical throne presses these States together; no iron chain of military power encircles them; they live and stand upon a government popular in its form, representative in its character, founded upon principles of equality, and so constructed, we hope, as to last for ever. In all its history it has been beneficent; it has trodden down no man's liberty; it has crushed no State. Its daily respiration is liberty and patriotism; its yet youthful veins are full of enterprise, courage, and honorable love of glory and renown. Large before, the country has now, by recent events, become vastly larger. This Republic now extends, with a vast breadth, across the whole continent. The two great seas of the world wash the one and the other shore. We realize, on a mighty scale, the beautiful description of the ornamental edging of the buckler of Achilles,—

> "Now the broad shield complete, the artist crowned
> With his last hand, and poured the ocean round:
> In living silver seemed the waves to roll,
> And beat the buckler's verge, and bound the whole."

CLAY

I

THE EMANCIPATION OF SOUTH AMERICA [1]
(1818)

Born in 1777, died in 1852; elected to the United States Senate in 1806, and again in 1810; elected to Congress in 1811–21, and again in 1823–25, serving three terms as Speaker; Peace Commissioner at Ghent in 1814; defeated for the Presidency in 1824; Secretary of State in 1825; elected United States Senator in 1831 and again in 1849; defeated for the Presidency in 1832 and in 1844; chief author of the compromises of 1820 and 1850.

SPAIN has undoubtedly given us abundant and just cause for war. But it is not every cause of war that should lead to war. War is one of those dreadful scourges that so shakes the foundation of society, overturns or changes the character of governments, interrupts or destroys the pursuits of private happiness, brings, in short, misery and wretchedness in so many forms, and at last is, in its issue, so doubtful and hazardous that nothing but dire necessity can justify an appeal to arms. If we are to have war with Spain, I have, however, no hesitation in saying that no mode of bringing it about could be less fortunate than that of seizing, at this time, upon her adjoining province. There was a time, under certain circumstances, when we might have oc-

---

[1] From a speech in the House of Representatives, March 24, 1818.

cupied East Florida with safety; had we then taken it, our posture in the negotiation with Spain would have been totally different from what it is.

But we have permitted that time, not with my consent, to pass by unimproved. If we were now to seize upon Florida after a great change in those circumstances, and after declaring our intention to acquiesce in the procrastination desired by Spain, in what light should we be viewed by foreign powers—particularly Great Britain? We have already been accused of inordinate ambition, and of seeking to aggrandize ourselves by an extension, on all sides, of our limits. Should we not, by such an act of violence, give color to the accusation? No, Mr. Chairman; if we are to be involved in a war with Spain, let us have the credit of disinterestedness. Let us put her yet more in the wrong. Let us command the respect which is never withheld from those who act a noble and generous part. I hope to communicate to the committee the conviction which I so strongly feel, that the adoption of the amendment which I intend to propose would not hazard, in the slightest degree, the peace of the country. But if that peace is to be endangered, I would infinitely rather it should be for our exerting the right appertaining to every State, of acknowledging the independence of another State, than for the seizure of a province, which sooner or later we must acquire.

In contemplating the great struggle in which Spanish America is now engaged, our attention is fixed first by the immensity and character of the country which Spain seeks again to subjugate. Stretching on the Pacific Ocean from about the fortieth degree of north latitude to about the fifty-fifth degree of south latitude, and extending from the mouth of the Rio del Norte (exclusive of East Florida), around the Gulf of Mexico and along the South Atlantic to near Cape Horn, it is nearly five thousand miles in length, and in some places nearly three thousand in breadth. Within this vast region we behold the most sublime and interesting objects of creation, the richest mines of the precious metals, and the choicest productions of the earth. We behold there a spectacle still more interesting and sublime—the glorious spectacle of eighteen millions of people struggling to burst their chains and to be free. When we take a little nearer and more detailed view, we perceive that nature has, as it were, ordained that this people and this country shall ultimately constitute several different nations.

Leaving the United States on the north, we come to New Spain, or the viceroyalty of Mexico on the south; passing by Guatemala, we reach the viceroyalty of New Granada, the late captain-generalship of Venezuela, and Guiana, lying on the east side of the Andes. Stepping over the Brazils, we arrive at the united provinces of La Plata, and crossing the Andes we find Chili on their west side, and, further north, the vice-royalty of Lima, or Peru. Each of these several parts is sufficient in itself in point of limits to constitute a powerful State; and, in point of population, that which has the smallest contains enough to make it respectable. Throughout all the extent of that great portion of the world which I have attempted thus hastily to describe, the spirit of revolt against the dominion of Spain has manifested itself. The Revolution has been attended with various degrees of success in the several parts of Spanish America. In some it has been already crowned, as I shall endeavor to show, with complete success, and in all I am persuaded that independence has struck such deep root, that the power of Spain can never eradicate it. What are the causes of this great movement?

Three hundred years ago, upon the ruins of the thrones of Montezuma and the Incas of Peru, Spain erected the most stupendous system of colonial despotism that the world has ever seen—the most vigorous, the most exclusive. The great principle and object of this system have been to render one of the largest portions of the world exclusively subservient, in all its faculties, to the interests of an inconsiderable spot in Europe. To effectuate this aim of her policy, she locked up Spanish America from all the rest of the world, and prohibited, under the severest penalties, any foreigner from entering any part of it. To keep the natives themselves ignorant of each other and of the strength and resources of the several parts of her American possessions, she next prohibited the inhabitants of one viceroyalty or government from visiting those of another; so that the inhabitants of Mexico, for example, were not allowed to enter the viceroyalty of New Granada. The agriculture of those vast regions was so regulated and restrained as to prevent all collision with the agriculture of the peninsula. Where nature, by the character and composition of the soil, has commanded, the abominable system of Spain has forbidden, the growth of certain articles. Thus the olive and the vine, to which Spanish America is so adapted, are prohibited wherever their culture can interfere with the olive and the vine peninsula.

The commerce of the country, in the direction and objects of the exports and imports, is also subjected to the narrow and selfish views of Spain, and fettered by the odious spirit of monopoly existing in Cadiz. She has sought, by scattering discord among the several castes of her American population, and by a debasing course of education, to perpetuate her oppression. Whatever concerns public law or the science of government, all writings upon political economy, or that tend to give vigor and freedom and expansion of the intellect, are prohibited. Gentlemen would be astonished by the long list of distinguished authors whom she proscribes, to be found in Depon's and other works. A main feature in her policy is that which constantly elevates the European and depresses the American character. Out of upward of seven · hundred and fifty viceroys and captains-general, whom she has appointed since the conquest of America, about eighteen only have been from the body of her American population. On all occasions, she seeks to raise and promote her European subjects, and to degrade and humiliate the Creoles. Wherever in America her sway extends, everything seems to pine and wither beneath its baneful influence. The richest regions of the earth, man, his happiness and his education, all the fine faculties of his soul, are regulated and modified and molded to suit the execrable purposes of an inexorable despotism.

Such is the brief and imperfect picture of the state of things in Spanish America in 1808, when the famous transactions of Bayonne occurred. The king of Spain and the Indies (for Spanish America has always constituted an integral part of the Spanish Empire) abdicated his throne and became a voluntary captive. Even at this day one does not know whether he should most condemn the baseness and perfidy of the one party, or despise the meanness and imbecility of the other. If the obligation of obedience and allegiance existed on the part of the Colonies to the king of Spain, it was founded on the duty of protection which he owed them. By disqualifying himself for the performance of this duty, they became released from that obligation. The monarchy was dissolved, and each integral part had a right to seek its own happiness by the institution of any new government adapted to its wants. Joseph Bonaparte, the successor de facto of Ferdinand, recognized this right on the part of the Colonies, and recommended them to establish their independence.

Thus upon the ground of strict right, upon the footing of a mere legal question, governed by forensic rules, the Colonies, being absolved by the acts of the parent country from the duty of subjection to it, had an indisputable right to set up for themselves. But I take a broader and a bolder position. I maintain that an oppressed people are authorized, whenever they can, to rise and break their fetters. This was the great principle of the English Revolution. It was the great principle of our own. Vattel, if authority were wanting, expressly supports this right. We must pass sentence of condemnation upon the founders of our liberty, say that you were rebels, traitors, and that we are at this moment legislating without competent powers, before we can condemn the cause of Spanish America. Our Revolution was mainly directed against the mere theory of tyranny. We had suffered but comparatively little; we had, in some respects, been kindly treated; but our intrepid and intelligent fathers saw, in the usurpation of the power to levy an inconsiderable tax, the long train of oppressive acts that were to follow. They rose; they breasted the storm;

they achieved our freedom. Spanish America for centuries has been doomed to the practical effects of an odious tyranny. If we were justified, she is more than justified.

In the establishment of the independence of Spanish America, the United States have the deepest interest. I have no hesitation in asserting my firm belief that there is no question in the foreign policy of this country, which has ever arisen, or which I can conceive as ever occurring, in the decision of which we have had or can have so much at stake. This interest concerns our politics, our commerce, our navigation. There can not be a doubt that Spanish America, once independent, whatever may be the form of government established in its several parts, these governments will be animated by an American feeling, and guided by an American policy. They will obey the laws of the system of the new world, of which they will compose a part, in contradistinction to that of Europe. Without the influence of that vortex in Europe, the balance of power between its several parts, the preservation of which has often drenched Europe in blood, America is sufficiently remote to contemplate the new wars which are to afflict that quarter of the globe, as a calm if not a cold and indifferent spectator. In relation to those wars, the several parts of America will generally stand neutral. And as, during the period when they rage, it will be important that a liberal system of neutrality should be adopted and observed, all America will be interested in maintaining and enforcing such a system. The independence of Spanish America, then, is an interest of primary consideration.

But it is sometimes said that they are too ignorant and too superstitious to admit of the existence of free government. This charge of ignorance is often urged by persons themselves actually ignorant of the real condition of that people. I deny the alleged fact of ignorance; I deny the inference from that fact, if it were true, that they want capacity for free government. And I refuse assent to the further conclusion if the fact were true, and the inference just, that we are to be indifferent to their fate. All the writers of the most established authority, Depons, Humboldt, and others, concur in assigning to the people of Spanish America great quickness, genius, and particular aptitude for the acquisition of the exact sciences, and others which they have been allowed to cultivate. In astronomy, geology, mineralogy, chemistry, botany, and so forth, they are allowed to make distinguished proficiency. They justly boast of their Abzate, Velasques, and Gama, and other illustrious contributors to science. They have nine universities, and in the City of Mexico, it is affirmed by Humboldt, there are more solid scientific establishments than in any city even of North America. I would refer to the message of the supreme director of La Plata, which I shall hereafter have occasion to use for another purpose, as a model of fine composition of a State paper, challenging a comparison with any, the most celebrated, that ever issued from the pens of Jefferson or Madison.

It is the doctrine of thrones that man is too ignorant to govern himself. Their partizans assert his incapacity, in reference to all nations; if they can not command universal assent to the proposition, it is then demanded to particular nations; and our pride and our presumption too often make converts of us. I contend, that it is to arraign the dispositions of Providence Himself, to suppose that He has created beings incapable of governing themselves, and to be trampled on by kings. Self-government is the natural government of man, and for proof I refer to the aborigines of our own land. Were I to speculate in hypotheses unfavorable to human liberty, my speculations should be founded rather upon the vices, refinements, or density of population. Crowded together in compact masses, even if they were philosophers, the contagion of the passions is communicated and caught, and the effect too often, I admit, is the overthrow of liberty. Dispersed over such an immense space as that on which the people of Spanish America are spread, their physical, and I believe, also, their moral condition, both favor their liberty.

With regard to their superstition, they worship the same God with us. Their prayers are offered up in their temples to the same Redeemer whose intercession we expect to save us. Nor is there anything in the Catholic religion unfavorable to freedom. All religions united with government are more or less inimical to liberty. All, separated from government, are compatible with liberty. If the people of Spanish America have not already gone as far in religious toleration as we have, the difference in their condition from ours should not be forgotten. Everything is progressive; and, in time, I hope to see them imitating in this respect our example. But grant that the people of Spanish America are ignorant and incompetent for free government, to whom is that ignorance to be ascribed? Is it not to the execrable system of Spain, which she seeks again to establish and to perpetuate? So far from chilling our hearts, it ought to increase our solicitude for unfortunate brethren. It ought to animate us to desire the redemption of the minds and bodies of unborn millions from the brutifying effects of a system whose tendency is to stifle the faculties of the soul and to degrade man to the level of beasts. I would invoke the spirits of our departed fathers. Was it for yourselves only that you nobly fought? No, no! It was the chains that were forging for your posterity that made you fly to arms, and, scattering the elements of these chains to the winds, you transmitted to us the rich inheritance of liberty.

II

HIS ATTACK ON JACKSON [1]
(1834)

NEVER, Mr. President, have I known or read of an administration which expires with so much agony, and so little composure and resignation, as that which now unfortunately has the control of public affairs in this country. It exhibits a state of mind, feverish, fretful, and fidgety, bounding recklessly from one desperate expedient to another, without any sober or settled purpose. Ever since the dog-days of last summer, it has been making a succession of the most extravagant plunges, of which the extraordinary cabinet paper, a sort of appeal from a descending cabinet to the people, was the first; and the protest, a direct appeal from the Senate to the people, is the last and the worst.

A new philosophy has sprung up within a few years past, called phrenology. There is, I believe, something in it, but not quite as much as its ardent followers proclaim. According to its doctrines, the leading passion, propensity, and characteristics of every man are developed in his physical conformation, chiefly in the structure of his head. Gall and Spurzheim, its founders, or most eminent propagators, being dead, I re-

[1] From a speech in the United States Senate, on April 30, 1834.

gret that neither of them can examine the head of our illustrious chief magistrate. But if it could be surveyed by Doctor Caldwell, of Transylvania University, I am persuaded that he would find the organ of destructiveness prominently developed.

Except an enormous fabric of executive power for himself, the president has built up nothing, constructed nothing, and will leave no enduring monument of his administration. He goes for destruction, universal destruction; and it seems to be his greatest ambition to efface and obliterate every trace of the wisdom of his predecessors. He has displayed this remarkable trait throughout his whole life, whether in private walks or in the public service. He signally and gloriously exhibited that peculiar organ when contending against the enemies of his country, in the Battle of New Orleans. For that brilliant exploit, no one has ever been more ready than myself to award him all due honor. At the head of our armies was his appropriate position, and most unfortunate for his fame was the day when he entered on the career of administration as the chief executive officer. He lives by excitement, perpetual, agitating excitement, and would die in a state of perfect repose and tranquillity. He has never been without some subject of attack, either in individuals, or in masses, or in institutions.

I, myself, have been one of his favorites, and I do not know but that I have recently recommended myself to his special regard. During his administration this has been his constant course. The Indians and Indian policy, internal improvements, the colonial trade, the Supreme Court, Congress, the banks, have successively experienced the attacks of his haughty and imperious spirit. And if he tramples the bank in the dust, my word for it, we shall see him quickly in chase of some new subject of his vengeance. This is the genuine spirit of conquerors and of conquest. It is said by the biographer of Alexander the Great that, after he had completed his Asiatic conquests, he seemed to sigh because there were no more worlds for him to subdue; and, finding himself without further employment for his valor or his arms, he turned within himself to search the means to gratify his insatiable thirst of glory. What sort of conquest he achieved of himself, the same biographer tragically records.

Already has the president singled out and designated, in the Senate of the United States, the new object of his hostile pursuit; and the protest, which I am now to consider, is his declaration of war. What has provoked it? The Senate, a component part of the Congress of the United States, at its last adjournment, left the Treasury of the United States in the safe custody of the persons and places assigned by law to keep it. Upon reassembling, it found the treasure removed; some of its guardians displaced; all, remaining, brought under the immediate control of the president's sole will; and the president having free and unobstructed access to the public money. The Senate believes that the purse of the nation is, by the Constitution and laws, intrusted to the exclusive legislative care of Congress. It has dared to avow and express this opinion, in a resolution adopted on the twenty-eighth of March last. That resolution was preceded by a debate of three months' duration, in the progress of which the able and zealous supporters of the executive in the Senate were attentively heard. Every argument which their ample resources, or those of the members of the executive, could supply was listened to with respect, and duly weighed. After full deliberation, the Senate expressed its conviction that the executive had violated the Constitution and laws. It cautiously refrained in the resolution from all examination into the motives or intention of the executive; it ascribed no bad ones to him; it restricted itself to a simple declaration of its solemn belief that the Constitution and laws had been violated. This is the extent of the offense of the Senate. This is what it has done to excite the executive indignation and to bring upon it the infliction of a denunciatory protest.

But, I would ask, in what tone, temper, and spirit does the president come to the Senate? As a great State culprit who has been arraigned at the bar of justice, or sentenced as guilty? Does he manifest any of those compunctious

visitings of conscience which a guilty violator
of the Constitution and laws of the land ought
to feel? Does he address himself to a high
court with the respect, to say nothing of hu-
mility, which a person accused or convicted
would naturally feel? No, no. He comes as
if the Senate were guilty, as if he were in the
judgment-seat, and the Senate stood accused before him. He arraigns the Senate; puts it upon
trial; condemns it; he comes as if he felt himself
elevated far above the Senate, and beyond all
reach of the law, surrounded by unapproachable
impunity. He who professes to be an innocent
and injured man gravely accuses the Senate,
and modestly asks it to put upon its own record
his sentence of condemnation! When before did
the arraigned or convicted party demand of the
court which was to try, or had condemned him,
to enter upon their records a severe denuncia-
tion of their own conduct? The president presents himself before the Senate, not in the garb
of suffering innocence, but in imperial and royal
costume—as a dictator, to rebuke a refractory
Senate; to command it to record his solemn protest; to chastise it for disobedience.

> "The hearts of princes kiss obedience,
> So much they love it; but to stubborn spirits
> They swell, and grow as terrible as storms."

The president exhibits great irritation and
impatience at the presumptuousness of a resolu-

tion, which, without the imputation of any bad intention or design, ventures to allege that he has violated the Constitution and laws. His constitution and official infallibility must not be questioned. To controvert it is an act of injustice, inhumanity, and calumny. He is treated as a criminal, and, without summons, he is prejudged, condemned, and sentenced. Is the president scrupulously careful of the memory of the dead, or the feelings of the living, in respect to violations of the Constitution? If a violation by him implies criminal guilt, a violation by them can not be innocent and guiltless.

And how has the president treated the memory of the immortal Father of his Country?—that great man, who, for purity of purpose and character, wisdom and moderation, unsullied virtue and unsurpassed patriotism, is without competition in past history or among living men, and whose equal we scarcely dare hope will ever be again presented as a blessing to mankind. How has he been treated by the president? Has he not again and again pronounced that, by approving the bill chartering the first Bank of the United States, Washington violated the Constitution of his country? That violation, according to the president, included volition and design, was prompted by improper motives, and was committed with an unlawful intent. It was the more inexcusable in Washington, because he assisted and presided in the convention which formed the Constitution. If it be unjust to arraign, try unheard, and condemn as guilty, a living man filling an exalted office, with all the splendor, power, and influence which that office possesses, how much more cruel is it to disturb the sacred and venerated ashes of the illustrious dead, who can raise no voice and make no protest against the imputation of high crime!

What has been the treatment of the president toward that other illustrious man, yet spared to us, but who is lingering upon the very verge of eternity? Has he abstained from charging the Father of the Constitution with criminal intent in violating the Constitution? Mr. Madison, like Washington, assisted in the formation of the Constitution; was one of its ablest expounders and advocates; and was opposed, on constitutional ground, to the first Bank of the United States. But yielding to the force of circumstances, and especially to the great principle, that the peace and stability of human society require that a controverted question, which has been finally settled by all the departments of government by long acquiescence, and by the people themselves, should not be open to perpetual dispute and disturbance, he approved the bill chartering the present Bank of the United States. Even the name of James Madison, which is but another for purity, patriotism, profound learning, and enlightened experience, can not escape the imputations of his present successor.

And, lastly, how often has he charged Congress itself with open violations of the Constitution? Times almost without number. During the present session he has sent in a message, in regard to the land bill, in which he has charged it with an undisguised violation. A violation so palpable that it is not even disguised, and must, therefore, necessarily imply a criminal intent. Sir, the advisers of the president, whoever they are, deceive him and themselves. They have vainly supposed that, by an appeal to the people, and an exhibition of the wounds of the president, they could enlist the sympathies and the commiseration of the people—that the name of Andrew Jackson would bear down the Senate and all opposition. They have yet to learn, what they will soon learn, that even a good and responsible name may be used so frequently, as an indorser, that its credit and the public confidence in its solidity have been seriously impaired. They mistake the intelligence of the people, who are not prepared to see and sanction the president putting forth indiscriminate charges of a violation of the Constitution against whomsoever he pleases, and exhibiting unmeasured rage and indignation when his own infallibility is dared to be questioned.

III

ON HIS OWN COMPROMISE MEASURES[1]
(1850)

WAS there ever a nation upon which the sun of heaven has shone which has exhibited so much of prosperity as our own? At the commencement of this government, our population amounted to about four millions. It has now reached upwards of twenty millions. Our territory was limited chiefly and principally to that bordering upon the Atlantic Ocean, and that which includes the southern shores of the interior lakes of our country. Our territory now extends from the northern provinces of Great Britain to the Rio Grande and the Gulf of Mexico; from the Atlantic Ocean on the one side to the Pacific on the other—the largest extent of territory under one government existing upon earth, with only two solitary exceptions. Our tonnage, from being nothing, has risen to a magnitude and amount to rival that of the nation

[1] From his speech in the United States Senate on February 6, 7, 1850. The attendance of the public on that day in the Senate was so great that the outer passages to the Senate-chamber were thronged with a crowd making such noise that Clay could not be heard inside. The passages were then cleared by direction of the president of the Senate. When Clay had finished his speech, Schurz says, "a great throng of friends—men, women, and children—rushed toward him to shake his hand and to kiss him."

which has been proudly called the mistress of the ocean.

We have gone through many wars; one with that very nation from whom in 1776 we broke off, as weak and feeble colonies, when we asserted our independence as a member of the family of nations. And, sir, we came out of that struggle—unequal as it was, armed as she was at all points in consequence of the long struggles of Europe, and unarmed as we were at all points, in consequence of the habits and nature of our country and its institutions—we came out of that war without the loss of any honor whatever; we emerged from it gloriously. In every Indian war—we have been engaged in many of them—our arms have been triumphant, and without speaking at all as to the causes of the recent war with Mexico, whether they were right or wrong, and abstaining from the expression of any opinion as to the justice or propriety of the war when it commenced, all must unite in respect to the gallantry of our arms and the glory of our triumphs.

There is no page—there are no pages of history which record more brilliant successes. With respect to the one in command of an important portion of our army, I need say nothing in praise of him who has been borne by the voice of his country to the highest station in it, mainly on account of his glorious military career.[1] But of another military commander, less fortunate

[1] Zachary Taylor, then president.

in other respects, I must take the opportunity of saying that for skill, for science, for strategy, for bold and daring fighting, for chivalry of individuals and of masses, that portion of the Mexican War which was conducted by the gallant Scott, as chief commander, stands unrivaled either by the deeds of Cortes himself or by those of any other commander in ancient or modern times.

Our prosperity is unbounded. Nay, Mr. President, I sometimes fear that it is the very wantonness of our prosperity that leads us to these threatening ills of the moment—that restlessness and these erratic schemes throughout the whole country, some of which have even found their way into legislative halls. We want, I fear, the chastising wand of heaven to bring us back to a sense of the immeasurable benefits and blessings which have been bestowed upon us by providence. At this moment, with the exception of here and there a particular department in the manufacturing business of the country, all are prosperous and happy—both the rich and the poor. Our nation has grown to a magnitude in power and in greatness to command the respect, if it does not call for the apprehensions, of all the powers of the earth with which we can come into contact. Sir, do I depict with colors too lively the prosperity which has resulted to us from the operation of the Constitution under which we live? Have I exaggerated in any degree?

Such is the Union, and such are its glorious fruits. We are told now, and it is rung throughout this entire country, that the Union is threatened with subversion and destruction. Well, the first question which naturally arises is, supposing the Union to be dissolved—having all the causes of grievance which are complained of —how far will dissolution furnish a remedy for those grievances? If the Union is to be dissolved for any existing causes, it will be dissolved because slavery is interdicted or not allowed to be introduced into the ceded territories; because slavery is threatened to be abolished in the District of Columbia; and because fugitive slaves are not returned, as in my opinion they ought to be, and restored to their masters. These, I believe, will be the causes, if there be any causes, which can lead to the direful event to which I have referred.

Well, now, let us suppose that the Union has been dissolved. What remedy does it furnish for the grievances complained of in its united condition? Will you be able to push slavery into the ceded Territories? How are you to do it, supposing the North—all the States north of the Potomac, and which are opposed to it—in possession of the navy and army of the United States? Can you expect, if there is a dissolution of the Union, that you can carry slavery into California and New Mexico? You can not dream of such a purpose. If it were abolished in the District of Columbia, and the Union were dissolved, would the dissolution of the Union restore slavery in the District of Columbia? Are you safer in the recovery of your fugitive slaves, in a state of dissolution or of severance of the Union, than you are in the Union itself?

But, I must take occasion to say that, in my opinion, there is no right on the part of one or more of the States to secede from the Union. War and the dissolution of the Union are identical and inseparable. There can be no dissolution of the Union except by consent or by war. No one can expect, in the existing state of things, that that consent would be given, and war is the only alternative by which a dissolution could be accomplished. And, Mr. President, if consent were given—if possibly we were to separate by mutual agreement and by a given line, in less than sixty days after such an agreement had been executed, war would break out between the free and slave-holding portions of this Union —between the two independent portions into which it would be erected in virtue of the act of separation.

Yes, sir, sixty days—in less than sixty days, I believe, our slaves from Kentucky would be fleeing over in numbers to the other side of the river, would be pursued by their owners, and the excitable and ardent spirits who would engage in the pursuit would be restrained by no sense of the rights which appertain to the independence of the other side of the river, supposing it, then, to be the line of separation. They would pursue their slaves; they would be repelled, and war would break out. In less than sixty days war would be blazing forth in every part of this now happy and peaceable land.

But how are you going to separate them? In my humble opinion, Mr. President, we should begin at least with three confederacies—the Confederacy of the North, the Confederacy of the Atlantic Southern States (the slave-holding States), and the Confederacy of the Valley of the Mississippi. My life upon it, sir, that vast population that has already concentrated, and will concentrate, upon the headquarters and tributaries of the Mississippi, will never consent that the mouth of that river shall be held subject to the power of any foreign State whatever. Such, I believe, would be the consequences of a dissolution of the Union. But other confederacies would spring up, from time to time, as dissatisfaction and discontent were disseminated over the country. There would be the Confederacy of the Lakes—perhaps the Confederacy of New England and of the Middle States.

I said that I thought that there was no right on the part of one or more of the States to secede from this Union. I think that the Constitution of the thirteen States was made, not merely for the generation which then existed, but for posterity, undefined, unlimited, permanent, and perpetual—for their posterity, and for every subsequent State which might come into the Union, binding themselves by that indissoluble bond. It is to remain for that posterity now and for ever. Like another of the great relations of private life, it was a marriage that no human authority can dissolve or divorce the parties from; and, if I may be allowed to refer to this same example in private life, let us say what man and wife say to each other: "We have mutual faults; nothing in the form of human beings can be perfect. Let us then be kind to each other, forbearing, conceding; let us live in happiness and peace."

Mr. President, I have said what I solemnly believe—that the dissolution of the Union and war are identical and inseparable; that they are convertible terms.

Such a war, too, as that would be, following the dissolution of the Union! Sir, we may search the pages of history, and none so furious, so bloody, so implacable, so exterminating, from the wars of Greece down, including those of the Commonwealth of England, and the Revolution of France—none, none of them raged with such violence, or was ever conducted with such bloodshed and enormities, as will that war which shall follow that disastrous event—if that event ever happens—of dissolution.

And what would be its termination? Standing armies and navies, to an extent draining the revenues of each portion of the disservered empire, would be created; exterminating wars would follow—not a war of two, nor three years, but of interminable duration—an exterminating war would follow, until some Philip or Alexander, some Cæsar or Napoleon, would rise to cut the Gordian knot, and solve the problem of the capacity of man for self-government, and crush the liberties of both the dissevered portions of this Union.

Can you doubt it? Look at history—consult the pages of all history, ancient or modern; look at human nature, look at the character of the contest in which you would be engaged in the supposition of a war following the dissolution of the Union, such as I have suggested— and I ask you if it is possible for you to doubt that the final but perhaps distant termination of the whole will be some despot treading down the liberties of the people?—that the final result will be the extinction of this last and glorious light, which is leading all mankind, who are gazing upon it, to cherish hope and anxious expectation that the liberty which prevails here will sooner or later be advanced throughout the civilized world?

Can you, Mr. President, lightly contemplate the consequences? Can you yield yourself to a torrent of passion, amid dangers which I have depicted in colors far short of what would be the reality, if the event should ever happen? I conjure gentlemen—whether from the South or the North—by all they hold dear in this world—by all their love of liberty—by all their veneration for their ancestors—by all their regard for posterity—by all their gratitude to Him who has bestowed upon them such unnumbered blessings—by all the duties which they owe to mankind, and all the duties they owe to themselves—by all these considerations I implore them to pause—solemnly to pause—at the edge of the precipice before the fearful and disastrous leap is taken in the yawning abyss below, which will inevitably lead to certain and irretrievable destruction.

And, finally, Mr. President, I implore, as the best blessing which heaven can bestow upon me on earth, that if the direful and sad event of the dissolution of the Union shall happen, I may not survive to behold the sad and heartrending spectacle.

CALHOUN

I

ON THE EXPUNGING RESOLUTION[1]
(1837)

Born in 1782, died in 1850; elected to Congress in 1811; Secretary of War in 1817; Vice-President in 1825; United States Senator in 1832–43; Secretary of State in 1844; again elected United States Senator in 1845.

THE gentleman from Virginia [Mr. Rives] says that the argument in favor of this Expunging Resolution has not been answered. Sir, there are some questions so plain that they can not be argued. Nothing can make them more plain; and this is one. No one, not blinded by party zeal, can possibly be insensible that the measure proposed is a violation of the Constitution. The Constitution requires the Senate to keep a journal; this resolution goes to expunge the journal. If you may expunge a part, you may expunge the whole; and if it is expunged, how is it kept? The Constitution says the journal shall be kept; this resolution says it shall be destroyed. It does the very thing which the Constitution declares shall not be done. That is the argument, the

[1] From a speech in the United States Senate in January, 1837. For Benton's speech on the same subject and the purport of the resolution, see volume eight.

whole argument. There is none other. Talk of precedents? and precedents drawn from a foreign country? They do not apply. No, sir. This is to be done, not in consequence of argument, but in spite of argument. I understand the case. I know perfectly well the gentlemen have no liberty to vote otherwise. They are coerced by an exterior power. They try, indeed, to comfort their conscience by saying that it is the will of the people, and the voice of the people. It is no such thing. We all know how these legislative returns have been obtained. It is by dictation from the White House. The president himself, with that vast mass of patronage which he wields, and the thousand expectations he is able to hold up, has obtained these votes of the State Legislatures; and this, forsooth, is said to be the voice of the people. The voice of the people! Sir, can we forget the scene which was exhibited in this Chamber when that Expunging Resolution was first introduced here? Have we forgotten the universal giving away of conscience, so that the senator from Missouri was left alone? I see before me senators who could not swallow that resolution; and has its nature changed since then? Is it any more constitutional now than it was then? Not at all. But executive power has interposed. Talk to me of the voice of the people! No, sir. It is the combination of patronage and power to coerce this body into a gross and palpable violation of the Constitution. Some individuals, I perceive, think to escape through the particular form in which this act is to be perpetrated. They tell us that the resolution on your records is not to be expunged, but is only to be endorsed "Expunged." Really, sir, I do not know how to argue against such contemptible sophistry. The occasion is too solemn for an argument of this sort. You are going to violate the Constitution, and you get rid of the infamy by a falsehood. You yourselves say that the resolution is expunged by your order. Yet you say it is not expunged. You put your act in express words. You record it and then turn round and deny it.

But what is the motive? What is the pretext for this enormity? Why, gentlemen tell us the Senate has two distinct consciences—a legislative conscience, and a judicial conscience. As a legislative body we have decided that the president has violated the Constitution. But gentlemen tell us that this is an impeachable offense; and, as we may be called to try it in our judicial capacity, we have no right to express the opinion. I need not show how inconsistent such a position is with the eternal, imprescriptible right of freedom of speech, and how utterly inconsistent it is with precedents drawn from the history of our British ancestors, where the same liberty of speech has for centuries been enjoyed. There is a shorter and more direct argument in reply. Gentlemen who take that position can not, according to their own showing, vote for this resolution; for if it is unconstitutional for us to record a resolution of condemnation, because we may afterward be called to try the case in a judicial capacity, then it is equally unconstitutional for us to record a resolution of acquittal. If it is unconstitutional for the Senate to declare before a trial that the president has violated the Constitution, it is equally unconstitutional to declare before a trial that he has not violated the Constitution. The same principle is involved in both. Yet, in the very face of this principle, gentlemen are here going to condemn their own act.

But why do I waste my breath? I know it is all utterly vain. The day is gone; night approaches, and night is suitable to the dark deed we meditate. There is a sort of destiny in this thing. The act must be performed; and it is an act which will tell on the political history of this country for ever. Other preceding violations of the Constitution (and they have been many and great) filled my bosom with indignation, but this fills it only with grief. Others were done in the heat of partizanship. Power was, as it were, compelled to support itself by seizing upon new instruments of influence and patronage; and there were ambitious and able men to direct the process. Such was the removal of the deposits, which the president seized upon by a new and unprecedented act of arbitrary power—an act which gave him ample means of rewarding friends and punishing enemies. Something may, perhaps, be pardoned to him in this matter on the old apology of tyrants—the plea of necessity.

But here there can be no such apology. Here no necessity can so much as be pretended. This act originates in pure, unmixed, personal idolatry. It is the melancholy evidence of a broken spirit, ready to bow at the feet of power. The former act was such a one as might have been perpetrated in the days of Pompey or Cæsar; but an act like this could never have been consummated by a Roman Senate until the times of Caligula and Nero.

II

ON THE CLAY COMPROMISE MEASURES[1]
(1850)

I HAVE, senators, believed from the first that the agitation of the subject of slavery would, if not prevented by some timely and effective measure, end in disunion. Entertaining this opinion, I have, on all proper occasions, endeavored to call the attention of both the two great parties which divide the country to adopt some measure to prevent so great a disaster, but without success. The agitation has been permit-

[1] This is perhaps the most famous of Calhoun's speeches. Being too ill to deliver it himself, he had carefully written it out, and on March 4, 1850, it was read by another senator, Calhoun being present. Calhoun died on March 31 of this year. Von Holst, Calhoun's biographer, writing of the scene in the Senate when the speech was delivered, says: "The galleries were hushed into the deepest silence by the extraordinary scene which had something of the impressive solemnity of a funeral ceremony." Mr. Schouler describes how Calhoun "listened to the delivery like some disembodied spirit,

ted to proceed with almost no attempt to resist it, until it has reached a point when it can no longer be disguised or denied that the Union is in danger. You have thus had forced upon you the greatest and gravest question that can ever come under your consideration: How can the Union be preserved?

To give a satisfactory answer to this mighty question, it is indispensable to have an accurate and thorough knowledge of the nature and the character of the cause by which the Union is endangered. Without such knowledge it is impossible to pronounce with any certainty, by what measure it can be saved; just as it would be impossible for a physican to pronounce in the case of some dangerous disease, with any certainty, by what remedy the patient could be saved, without similar knowledge of the nature and character of the cause which produce it. The first question, then, presented for consideration in the investigation I propose to make in order to obtain such knowledge is: What is it that has endangered the Union?

To this question there can be but one answer, —that the immediate cause is the almost univer-

reviewing the deeds of the flesh." "It was a strangely haunting spectacle," he adds. "The author turned half round and listened as tho all were new to him, moving not a muscle of his face, but keeping his immovable posture—pale, skinny, and emaciated that he was—his eyes partially closed, until the last words were uttered and the spell was broken." When the Senate adjourned, Von Holst says Calhoun, "supported cn the shoulders of two of his friends, tottered out of the Senate-chamber." Abridged.

sal discontent which pervades all the States composing the Southern section of the Union. This widely extended discontent is not of recent origin. It commenced with the agitation of the slavery question and has been increasing ever since. The next question, going one step further back, is: What has caused this widely diffused and almost universal discontent?

It is a great mistake to suppose, as is by some, that it originated with demagogs who excited the discontent with the intention of aiding their personal advancement, or with the disappointed ambition of certain politicians who resorted to it as the means of retrieving their fortunes. On the contrary, all the great political influences of the section were arrayed against excitement, and exerted to the utmost to keep the people quiet. The great mass of the people of the South were divided, as in the other section, into Whigs and Democrats. The leaders and the presses of both parties in the South were very solicitous to prevent excitement and to preserve quiet; because it was seen that the effects of the former would necessarily tend to weaken, if not destroy, the political ties which united them with their respective parties in the other section.

Those who know the strength of party ties will readily appreciate the immense force which this cause exerted against agitation and in favor of preserving quiet. But, great as it was, it was not sufficient to prevent the widespread discontent which now pervades the section.

No; some cause far deeper and more powerful than the one supposed must exist, to account for discontent so wide and deep. The question then recurs: What is the cause of this discontent? It will be found in the belief of the people of the Southern States, as prevalent as the discontent itself, that they can not remain, as things now are, consistently with honor and safety, in the Union. The next question to be considered is: What has caused this belief?

One of the causes is, undoubtedly, to be traced to the long-continued agitation of the slave question on the part of the North, and the many aggressions which they have made on the rights of the South during the time. I will not enumerate them at present, as it will be done hereafter in its proper place.

There is another lying back of it—with which this is intimately connected—that may be regarded as the great and primary cause. This is to be found in the fact that the equilibrium between the two sections in the government as it stood when the Constitution was ratified and the government put in action has been destroyed. At that time there was nearly a perfect equilibrium between the two, which afforded ample means to each to protect itself against the aggression of the other; but, as it now stands, one section has the exclusive power of controlling the government, which leaves the other without any adequate means of protecting itself against its encroachment and oppression.

The result of the whole is to give the Northern section a predominance in every department of the government, and thereby concentrate in it the two elements which constitute the federal government: a majority of States, and a majority of their population, estimated in federal numbers. Whatever section concentrates the two in itself possesses the control of the entire government.

But we are just at the close of the sixth decade and the commencement of the seventh. The census is to be taken this year, which must add greatly to the decided preponderance of the North in the House of Representatives and in the Electoral College. The prospect is, also, that a great increase will be added to its present preponderance in the Senate, during the period of the decade, by the addition of new States. Two Territories, Oregon and Minnesota, are already in progress, and strenuous efforts are making to bring in three additional States from the Territory recently conquered from Mexico; which, if successful, will add three other States in a short time to the Northern section, making five States, and increasing the present number of its States from fifteen to twenty, and of its senators from thirty to forty.

On the contrary, there is not a single Territory in progress in the Southern section, and no certainty that any additional State will be added to it during the decade. The prospect then is, that the two sections in the Senate, should the efforts now made to exclude the South from the newly acquired Territories succeed, will stand, before the end of the decade, twenty Northern States to fourteen Southern (considering Delaware as neutral), and forty Northern senators to twenty-eight Southern. This great increase of senators, added to the great increase of members of the House of Representatives and the Electoral College on the part of the North, which must take place under the next decade, will effectually and irretrievably destroy the equilibrium which existed when the government commenced.

Had this destruction been the operation of time without the interference of government, the South would have had no reason to complain; but such was not the fact. It was caused by the legislation of this government, which was appointed as the common agent of all and charged with the protection of the interests and security of all.

The legislation by which it has been effected may be classed under three heads: The first is that series of acts by which the South has been excluded from the common territory belonging to all the States as members of the federal Union—which have had the effect of extending vastly the portion allotted to the Northern section, and restricting within narrow limits the portion left the South. The next consists in adopting a system of revenue and disbursements by which an undue proportion of the burden of taxation has been imposed upon the South, and an undue proportion of its proceeds appropriated to the North. And the last is a system of political measures by which the original character of the government has been radically changed. I propose to bestow upon each of these, in the order they stand, a few remarks, with the view of showing that it is owing to the action of this government that the equilibrium between the two sections has been destroyed, and the whole powers of the system centered in a sectional majority.

I have not included the territory recently acquired by the treaty with Mexico. The North is making the most strenuous efforts to appropriate the whole to herself, by excluding the South from every foot of it. If she should succeed, it will add to that from which the South has already been excluded 526,078 square miles, and would increase the whole which the North has appropriated to herself to 1,764,023, not including the portion that she may succeed in excluding us from in Texas. To sum up the whole, the United States, since they declared their independence, have acquired 2,373,046 square miles of territory, from which the North will have excluded the South, if she should succeed in monopolizing the newly-acquired Territories, about three-fourths of the whole, leaving to the South but about one-fourth. Such is the first and great cause that has destroyed the equilibrium between the two sections in the government

The next is the system of revenue and disbursements which has been adopted by the government. It is well known that the government has derived its revenue mainly from duties on imports. I shall not undertake to show that such duties must necessarily fall mainly on the exporting States, and that the South, as the great exporting portion of the Union, has in reality paid vastly more than her due proportion of the revenue; because I deem it unnecessary, as the subject has on so many occasions been fully discussed. Nor shall I, for the same reason, undertake to show that a far greater portion of the revenue has been disbursed in the North, than its due share; and that the joint effect of these causes has been to transfer a vast amount from South to North, which, under an equal system of revenue and disbursements, would not have been lost to her. If to this be added that many of the duties were imposed, not for revenue but for protection—that is, intended to put money, not in the Treasury, but directly into the pocket of the manufacturers—some conception may be formed of the immense amount which in the long course of sixty years has been transferred from South to North. There are no data by which it can be estimated with any certainty; but it is safe to say that it amounts to hundreds of millions of dollars. Under the most moderate estimate it would be sufficient to add greatly to the wealth of the North, and thus greatly increase her population by attracting immigration from all quarters to that section.

This, combined with the great primary cause, amply explains why the North has acquired a preponderance in every department of the government by its disproportionate increase of population and States. The former, as has been shown, has increased, in fifty years, 2,400,000 over that of the South. This increase of population during so long a period is satisfactorily accounted for by the number of immigrants, and the increase of their descendants, which have been attracted to the Northern section from Europe and the South, in consequence of the advantages derived from the causes assigned. If they had not existed—if the South had retained all the capital which has been extracted from her by the fiscal action of the government; and if it had not been excluded by the Ordinance of 1787 and the Missouri Compromise, from the region lying between the Ohio and the Mississippi Rivers, and between the Mississippi and the Rocky Mountains north of 36° 30′—it scarcely admits of a doubt that it would have divided the immigration with the North, and by retaining her own people would have at least equaled the North in population under the census of 1840, and probably under that about to be taken. She would also, if she had retained her equal rights in those territories, have maintained an equality in the number of States with the North, and have preserved the equilibrium between the two sections that existed at the commencement of the government. The loss, then, of the equilibrium is to be attributed to the action of this government.

There is a question of vital importance to the Southern section, in reference to which the views and feelings of the two sections are as opposite and hostile as they can possibly be. I refer to the relation between the two races in the Southern section, which constitutes a vital portion of her social organization. Every portion of the North entertains views and feelings more or less hostile to it. Those most opposed and hostile regard it as a sin, and consider themselves under the most sacred obligation to use every effort to destroy it.

Indeed, to the extent that they conceive that they have power, they regard themselves as implicated in the sin, and responsible for not suppressing it by the use of all and every means. Those less opposed and hostile regard it as a crime—an offense against humanity, as they call it and, altho not so fanatical, feel themselves bound to use all efforts to effect the same object; while those who are least opposed and hostile regard it as a blot and a stain on the character of what they call the "nation," and feel themselves accordingly bound to give it no countenance or support. On the contrary, the Southern section regards the relation as one which can not be destroyed without subjecting the two races to the greatest calamity, and the section to poverty, desolation, and wretchedness; and accordingly they feel bound by every consideration of interest and safety to defend it.

Unless something decisive is done, I again ask, What is to stop this agitation before the great and final object at which it aims—the abolition of slavery in the States—is consummated? Is it, then, not certain that if something is not done to arrest it, the South will be forced to choose between abolition and secession? Indeed, as events are now moving, it will not require the South to secede in order to dissolve the Union. Agitation will of itself effect it, of which its past history furnishes abundant proof —as I shall next proceed to show.

It is a great mistake to suppose that disunion can be effected by a single blow. The cords which bind these States together in one common Union are far too numerous and powerful for that. Disunion must be the work of time. It is only through a long process, and successively, that the cords can be snapped until the whole fabric falls asunder. Already the agitation of the slavery question has snapped some of the most important, and has greatly weakened all the others.

If the agitation goes on, the same force, acting with increased intensity, as has been shown, will finally snap every cord, when nothing will be left to hold the States together except force. But surely that can with no propriety of language be called a Union when the only means by which the weaker is held connected with the stronger portion is force. It may, indeed, keep them connected; but the connection will partake much more of the character of subjugation on the part of the weaker to the stronger than the union of free, independent, and sovereign States in one confederation, as they stood in the early stages of the government, and which only is worthy of the sacred name of Union.

Having now, senators, explained what it is that endangers the Union, and traced it to its cause, and explained its nature and character, the question again recurs, How can the Union be saved? To this I answer, there is but one way by which it can be, and that is by adopting such measures as will satisfy the States belonging to the Southern section that they can remain in the Union consistently with their honor and their safety. There is, again, only one way by which this can be effected, and that is by removing the causes by which this belief has been produced. Do this, and discontent will cease, harmony and kind feelings between the sections be restored, and every apprehension of danger to the Union removed. The question, then, is, How can this be done? There is but one way by which it can with any certainty; and that is by a full and final settlement, on the principle of justice, of all the questions at issue between the two sections. The South asks for justice, simple justice, and less she ought not to take. She has no compromise to offer but the Constitution, and no concession or surrender to make. She has already surrendered so much that she has little left to surrender. Such a settlement would go to the root of the evil, and remove all cause of discontent, by satisfying the South that she could remain honorably and safely in the Union, and thereby restore the harmony and fraternal feelings between the sections which existed anterior to the Missouri agitation. Nothing else can, with any certainty, finally and for ever settle the question at issue, terminate agitation, and save the Union.

But can this be done? Yes, easily; not by the weaker party, for it can of itself do nothing— not even protect itself—but by the stronger. The North has only to will it to accomplish it —to do justice by conceding to the South an equal right in the acquired territory, and to do her duty by causing the stipulations relative to fugitive slaves to be faithfully fulfilled—to cease the agitation of the slave question, and to provide for the insertion of a provision in the Constitution, by an amendment, which will restore to the South, in substance, the power she possessed of protecting herself before the equilibrium between the sections was destroyed by the action of this government. There will be no difficulty in devising such a provision—one that will protect the South, and which at the same time will improve and strengthen the government instead of impairing and weakening it.

But will the North agree to this? It is for

her to answer the question. But, I will say, she can not refuse if she has half the love of the Union which she professes to have, or without justly exposing herself to the charge that her love of power and aggrandizement is far greater than her love of the Union. At all events, the responsibility of saving the Union rests on the North, and not on the South. The South can not save it by any act of hers, and the North may save it without any sacrifice whatever, unless to do justice and to perform her duties under the Constitution should be regarded by her as a sacrifice.

It is time, senators, that there should be an open and manly avowal on all sides as to what is intended to be done. If the question is not now settled, it is uncertain whether it ever can hereafter be; and we, as the representatives of the States of this Union regarded as governments, should come to a distinct understanding as to our respective views, in order to ascertain whether the great questions at issue can be settled or not. If you who represent the stronger portion, can not agree to settle them on the broad principle of justice and duty, say so; and let the States we both represent agree to separate and part in peace.

If you are unwilling we should part in peace, tell us so; and we shall know what to do when you reduce the question to submission or resistance. If you remain silent, you will compel us to infer by your acts what you intend. In that case California will become the test question. If you admit her under all the difficulties that oppose her admission, you compel us to infer that you intend to exclude us from the whole of the acquired Territories, with the intention of destroying irretrievably the equilibrium between the two sections. We should be blind not to perceive in that case that your real objects are power and aggrandizement, and infatuated, not to act accordingly.

I have now, senators, done my duty in expressing my opinions fully, freely, and candidly on this solemn occasion. In doing so I have been governed by the motives which have governed me in all the stages of the agitation of the slavery question since its commencement. I have exerted myself during the whole period to arrest it, with the intention of saving the Union if it could be done; and if it could not, to save the section where it has pleased providence to cast my lot, and which I sincerely believe has justice and the Constitution on its side. Having faithfully done my duty to the best of my ability, both to the Union and my section, throughout this agitation, I shall have the consolation, let what will come, that I am free from all responsibility.

CORWIN

ON THE MEXICAN WAR [1]
(1847)

Born in 1794, died in 1865; elected to Congress in 1831; Governor of Ohio in 1840; United States Senator in 1845; Secretary of the Treasury in 1850; Member of Congress again in 1859; Minister to Mexico in 1861.

THE president has said he does not expect to hold Mexican territory by conquest. Why then conquer it? Why waste thousands of lives and millions of money fortifying towns and creating governments, if, at the end of the war, you retire from the graves of your soldiers and the desolated country of your foes, only to get money from Mexico for the expense of all your toil and sacrifice? Who ever heard, since Christianity was propagated among men, of a nation taxing its people, enlisting its young men, and marching off two thousand miles to fight a people merely to be paid for it in money? What is this but hunting a market for blood, selling the lives of your young men, marching them in regiments to be slaughtered and paid for like oxen and brute beasts?

Sir, this is, when stripped naked, that atro-

---

[1] From his speech to the United States Senate on February 11, 1847.

cious idea first promulgated in the president's message, and now advocated here, of fighting on till we can get our indemnity for the past as well as the present slaughter. We have chastised Mexico, and if it were worth while to do so, we have, I dare say, satisfied the world that we can fight.

Sir, I have no patience with this flagitious notion of fighting for indemnity, and this under the equally absurd and hypocritical pretense of securing an honorable peace. An honorable peace! If you have accomplished the objects of the war—if indeed you had an object which you dare to avow—cease to fight and you will have peace. Conquer your insane love of false glory, and you will "conquer a peace."

But now you have overrun half of Mexico, you have exasperated and irritated her people, you claim indemnity for all expenses incurred in doing this mischief and boldly ask her to give up New Mexico and California; and, as a bribe to her patriotism, seizing on her property, you offer three millions to pay the soldiers she has called out to repel your invasion on condition that she will give up to you at least one-third of her whole territory. This is the modest—I should say, the monstrous—proposition now before us as explained by the chairman of the committee on foreign relations [Mr. Sevier], who reported the bill. I can not now give my consent to this.

You may wrest provinces from Mexico by

war—you may hold them by the right of the strongest—you may rob her; but a treaty of peace to that effect with the people of Mexico, legitimately and freely made, you never will have! I thank God that it is so, as well for the sake of the Mexican people as ourselves; for, unlike the senator from Alabama [Mr. Bagby], I do not value the life of a citizen of the United States above the lives of a hundred thousand Mexican women and children—a rather cold sort of philanthropy, in my judgment. For the sake of Mexico, then, as well as our own country, I rejoice that it is an impossibility that you can obtain by treaty from her those territories under the existing state of things.

You have taken from Mexico one-fourth of her territory, and you now propose to run a line comprehending about another third, and for what? I ask, Mr. President, for what? What has Mexico got from you for parting with two-thirds of her domain? She has given you ample redress for every injury of which you have complained. She has submitted to the award of your commissioners, and up to the time of the rupture with Texas faithfully paid it. And for all that she has lost (not through or by you, but which loss has been your gain) what requital do we, her strong, rich, robust neighbor, make? Do we send our missionaries there "to point the way to heaven?" Or do we send the schoolmasters to pour daylight into her dark places, to aid her infant strength to conquer freedom and reap the fruit of the independence herself alone had won?

No, no, none of this do we! But we send regiments, storm towns, and our colonels prate of liberty in the midst of the solitudes their ravages have made. They proclaim the empty forms of social compact to a people bleeding and maimed with wounds received in defending their hearthstones against the invasion of these very men who shoot them down and then exhort them to be free.

What is the territory, Mr. President, which you propose to wrest from Mexico? It is consecrated to the heart of the Mexican by many a well-fought battle with his old Castilian master. His Bunker Hills, and Saratogas, and Yorktowns are there. The Mexican can say, "There I bled for liberty! and shall I surrender that consecrated home of my affections to the Anglo-Saxon invaders? What do they want with it? They have Texas already. They have possessed themselves of the territory between the Nueces and the Rio Grande. What else do they want? To what shall I point my children as memorials of that independence which I bequeath to them when those battle-fields shall have passed from my possession?"

Sir, had one come and demanded Bunker Hill of the people of Massachusetts, had England's lion ever showed himself there, is there a man over thirteen and under ninety who would not have been ready to meet him; is there a river on this continent that would not have run red with blood; is there a field but would have been piled high with the unburied bones of slaughtered Americans before these consecrated battle-fields of liberty should have been wrested from us? But this same American goes into a sister republic and says to poor, weak Mexico, "Give up your territory—you are unworthy to possess it—I have got one-half already—all I ask of you is to give up the other!"

Why, says the chairman of this committee on foreign relations, it is the most reasonable thing in the world! We ought to have the Bay of San Francisco. Why? Because it is the best harbor on the Pacific! It has been my fortune, Mr. President, to have practised a good deal in criminal courts in the course of my life, but I never yet heard a thief arraigned for stealing a horse plead that it was the best horse that he could find in the country! We want California. What for? Why, says the senator from Michigan, we will have it; and the senator from South Carolina, with a very mistaken view, I think, of policy, says you can not keep our people from going there.

Let them go and seek their happiness in whatever country or clime it pleases them. All I ask of them is, not to require this government to protect them with that banner consecrated to war waged for principles—eternal, enduring truth. Sir, it is not meet that our old flag should throw its protecting folds over expeditions for lucre or for land. But you still say you want room for your people. This has been the plea of every robber-chief from Nimrod to the present hour. I dare say, when Tamerlane descended from his throne built of seventy thousand human skulls, and marched his ferocious battalions to further slaughter, I dare say he said, "I want room."

Bajazet was another gentleman of kindred tastes and wants with us Anglo-Saxons—he "wanted room." Alexander, too, the mighty "Macedonian madman," when he wandered with his Greeks to the plains of India and fought a bloody battle on the very ground where recently England and the Sikhs engaged in strife for "room," was no doubt in quest of some California there. Many a Monterey had he to storm to get "room."

Sir, he made quite as much of that sort of history as you ever will. Mr. President, do you remember the last chapter in that history? It is soon read. Oh! I wish we could but understand its moral. Ammon's son (so was Alexander named), after all his victories, died drunk in Babylon! The vast empire he conquered to "get room" became the prey of the generals he had trained; it was disparted, torn to pieces, and so ended. Sir, there is a very significant appendix; it is this: The descendants of the Greeks—of Alexander's Greeks—are now governed by a descendant of Attila!

Sir, I have read in some account of your Battle

of Monterey, of a lovely Mexican girl, who, with the benevolence of an angel in her bosom and the robust courage of a hero in her heart, was busily engaged during the bloody conflict, amid the crash of falling houses, the groans of the dying, and the wild shriek of battle, in carrying water to slake the burning thirst of the wounded of either host. While bending over a wounded American soldier a cannon-ball struck her and blew her to atoms! Sir, I do not charge my brave, generous-hearted countrymen who fought that fight with this. No, no! We who send them —we who know that scenes like this, which might send tears of sorrow "down Pluto's iron cheek," are the invariable, inevitable attendants on war —we are accountable for this. And this—this is the way we are to be made known to Europe. This—this is to be the undying renown of free, republican America! "She has stormed a city —killed many of its inhabitants of both sexes —she has room!" So it will read. Sir, if this were our only history, then may God of His mercy grant that its volume may speedily come to a close.

Why is it, sir, that we, the United States, a people of yesterday compared with the older nations of the world, should be waging war for territory—for "room?" Look at your country, extending from the Alleghany Mountains to the Pacific Ocean, capable itself of sustaining in comfort a larger population than will be in the whole Union for one hundred years to come.

Over this vast expanse of territory your population is now so sparse that I believe we provided,
at the last session, a regiment of mounted men
to guard the mail from the frontier of Missouri
to the mouth of the Columbia; and yet you
persist in the ridiculous assertion, "I want
room." One would imagine, from the frequent
reiteration of the complaint, that you had a
bursting, teeming population, whose energy was
paralyzed, whose enterprise was crushed, for
want of space. Why should we be so weak or
wicked as to offer this idle apology for ravaging
a neighboring Republic? It will impose on no
one at home or abroad.

Do we not know, Mr. President, that it is
a law never to be repealed that falsehood shall
be short-lived? Was it not ordained of old that
truth only shall abide for ever? Whatever we
may say to-day, or whatever we may write in
our books, the stern tribunal of history will re-
view it all, detect falsehood, and bring us to
judgment before that posterity which shall bless
or curse us, as we may act now, wisely or otherwise. We may hide in the grave (which awaits
us all) in vain; we may hope there, like the
foolish bird that hides its head in the sand, in
the vain belief that its body is not seen; yet
even there this preposterous excuse of want of
"room" shall be laid bare and the quick-coming
future will decide that it was a hypocritical
pretense under which we sought to conceal the
avarice which prompted us to covet and to seize
by force that which was not ours.

Mr. President, this uneasy desire to augment our territory has depraved the moral sense and blunted the otherwise keen sagacity of our people. What has been the fate of all nations who have acted upon the idea that they must advance! Our young orators cherish this notion with a fervid but fatally mistaken zeal. They call it by the mysterious name of "destiny." "Our destiny," they say, is "onward," and hence they argue, with ready sophistry, the propriety of seizing upon any territory and any people that may lie in the way of our "fated" advance. Recently these progressives have grown classical; some assiduous student of antiquities has helped them to a patron saint. They have wandered back into the desolate Pantheon, and there, among the polytheistic relics of that "pale mother of dead empires,"[1] they have found a god whom these Romans, centuries gone by, baptized "Terminus."[2]

Sir, I have heard much and read somewhat of this gentleman Terminus. Alexander, of whom I have spoken, was a devotee of this divinity. We have seen the end of him and his empire. It was said to be an attribute of this god that he must always advance and never recede. So both republican and imperial Rome

---

[1] "Lone mother of dead empires," are Byron's exact words.

[2] Terminus, in Roman mythology, was the god who presided over the boundaries of States, and was represented without arms or legs, in order to indicate that he never gave up a place he had once occupied.

believed. It was, as they said, their destiny. And for a while it did seem to be even so. Roman Terminus did advance. Under the eagles of Rome he was carried from his home on the Tiber to the farthest East on the one hand, and to the far West, among the then barbarious tribes of western Europe, on the other.

But at length the time came when retributive justice had become "a destiny." The despised Gaul calls out the contemned Goth, and Attila with his Huns answers back the battle-shout to both. The "blue-eyed nations of the North," in succession or united, pour forth their countless hosts of warriors upon Rome and Rome's always-advancing god Terminus. And now the battle-ax of the barbarian strikes down the conquering eagle of Rome. Terminus at last recedes, slowly at first, but finally he is driven to Rome, and from Rome to Byzantium. Whoever would know the further fate of this Roman deity, so recently taken under the patronage of American democracy, may find ample gratification of his curiosity in the luminous pages of Gibbon's "Decline and Fall."

Such will find that Rome thought as you now think, that it was her destiny to conquer provinces and nations, and no doubt she sometimes said, as you say, "I will conquer a peace," and where now is she, the mistress of the world? The spider weaves his web in her palaces; the owl sings his watch-song in her towers. Teutonic power now lords it over the servile remnant, the miserable memento of old and once omnipotent Rome.

Sad, very sad, are the lessons which time has written for us. Through and in them all I see nothing but the inflexible execution of that old law which ordains as eternal that cardinal rule, "Thou shalt not covet thy neighbor's goods, nor anything which is his." Since I have lately heard so much about the dismemberment of Mexico I have looked back to see how, in the course of events, which some call "providence," it has fared with other nations who engaged in this work of dismemberment. I see that in the latter half of the eighteenth century three powerful nations, Russia, Austria, and Prussia, united in the dismemberment of Poland. They said, too, as you say, "It is our destiny." They "wanted room." Doubtless each of these thought, with his share of Poland, his power was too strong ever to fear invasion, or even insult. One had his California, another his New Mexico, and the third his Vera Cruz. Did they remain untouched and incapable of harm? Alas! no—far, very far, from it. Retributive justice must fulfil its destiny, too.

A very few years pass off, and we hear of a new man, a Corsican lieutenant, the self-named "armed soldier of democracy," Napoleon. He ravages Austria, covers her land with blood, drives the Northern Cæsar from his capital, and sleeps in his palace. Austria may now remember how her power trampled upon Poland.

Did she not pay dear, very dear, for her California?

But has Prussia no atonement to make? You see this same Napoleon, the blind instrument of providence, at work there. The thunders of his cannon at Jena proclaim the work of retribution for Poland's wrongs; and the success of the Great Frederick, the drill-sergeant of Europe, are seen flying across the sandy plain that surrounds their capital, right glad if they may escape captivity or death. But how fares it with the autocrat of Russia? Is he secure in his share of the spoils of Poland? No. Suddenly we see, sir, six hundred thousand armed men marching to Moscow. Does his Vera Cruz protect him now? Far from it. Blood, slaughter, desolation spread abroad over the land, and finally the conflagration of the old commercial metropolis of Russia closes the retribution she must pay for her share in the dismemberment of her weak and impotent neighbor.

Mr. President, a mind more prone to look for the judgments of heaven in the doings of men than mine, can not fail in this to see the providence of God. When Moscow burned, it seemed as if the earth was lighted up that the nations might behold the scene. As that mighty sea of fire gathered and heaved and rolled upward and yet higher till its flames licked the stars and fired the whole heavens, it did seem as tho the God of the nations was writing in characters of flame on the front of his throne that doom shall fall upon the strong nation which tramples in scorn upon the weak. And what fortune awaits him, the appointed executor of this work, when it was all done? He, too, conceived the notion that his destiny pointed onward to universal dominion. France was too small—Europe, he thought, should bow down before him.

But as soon as this idea took possession of his soul, he, too, becomes powerless. His Terminus must recede, too. Right there, while he witnessed the humiliation and doubtless meditated the subjugation of Russia, He who holds the winds in His fist gathered the snows of the north and blew them upon his six hundred thousand men; they fled—they froze—they perished. And now the mighty Napoleon, who has resolved on universal dominion, he, too, is summoned to answer for the violation of that ancient law, "Thou shalt not covet anything which is thy neighbor's." How is the mighty fallen! He, beneath whose proud footstep Europe trembled, he is now an exile at Elba, and now finally a prisoner on the rock of St. Helena, and there, on a barren island, in an unfrequented sea, in the crater of an extinguished volcano, there is the death-bed of the mighty conqueror. All his annexations have come to that! His last hour is now come, and he, the man of destiny, he who had rocked the world as with the throes of an earthquake, is now powerless, still—even as a beggar, so he died. On the wings of a tempest that raged with unwonted fury, up to the throne of the only Power that controlled him while he lived, went the fiery soul of that wonderful warrior, another witness to the existence of that eternal decree that they who do not rule in righteousness shall perish from the earth. He has found "room" at last.

And France,—she, too, has found "room." Her "eagles" now no longer scream along the banks of the Danube, the Po, and the Borysthenes. They have returned home, to their old eyrie, between the Alps, the Rhine, and the Pyrenees. So it shall be with yours. You may carry them to the loftiest peaks of the Cordilleras, they may wave with insolent triumph in the halls of the Montezumas, the armed men of Mexico may quail before them, but the weakest hand in Mexico, uplifted in prayer to the God of Justice, may call down against you a Power in the presence of which the iron hearts of your warriors shall be turned into ashes.

ALEXANDER H. STEPHENS

THE SOUTH AND THE PUBLIC DOMAIN [1]
(1850)

Born in 1812, died in 1883; elected to Congress in 1843-59; opposed
Secession in 1860; Vice-President of the Confederacy in 1861-65;
imprisoned in Boston Harbor from May to October, 1865; elected
United States Senator in 1866, but not seated; Member of Congress
in 1873-82; elected Governor of Georgia in 1883.

A PUBLIC domain has been acquired by the
common blood and common treasure of all, and
the South, which is charged with endeavoring
to control the government for its purposes, asks
nothing but that the common territory which
is the public property may be opened to the
entry and settlement and equal enjoyment of
all the citizens of every part of the Republic,
with their property of every description; while
it is the North which comes here and demands
that the whole of this common domain shall be
set apart exclusively for itself, or for itself and
such persons from the South as will strip themselves of a certain species of their property, and
conform their views to the policy of the North.
I submit it to every candid man in this House,
and to every intelligent and candid man in the
world, outside of the House, if this is not a fair

[1] From a speech in the House of Representatives, August 6, 1850.

statement of the question. The South asks no discrimination in her favor. It is the North that is seeking to obtain discriminations against her and her people. And who leads in this endeavor to control the action of the government for sectional objects? It is the gentleman himself who brings this charge against the South. Sir, I deny the charge, and repel it. And I tell that gentleman and the House if these agitations are not to cease until the South shall quietly and silently yield to these demands of the North, it is useless to talk of any amicable settlement of the matters in controversy. If that is the basis you propose, we need say nothing further about agreement or adjustment—upon those terms we can never settle. The people of the South have as much right to occupy, enjoy, and colonize these Territories with their property as the people of the North have with theirs. This is the basis upon which I stand, and the principles upon which it rests are as immutable as right and justice. They are the principles of natural law, founded in natural justice, as recognized by the ablest publicists who have written upon the laws of nations and the rights pertaining to conquests. These acquisitions belong to the whole people of the United States, as conquerors. They hold them under the Constitution and the general government as common property in a corporate capacity.

Under our Constitution the power of making

regulations for the enjoyment of the common domain devolves upon Congress—the common agent of all the parties interested in it. In the execution of this trust it is the duty of Congress to pass all laws for an equal and just participation in it. And far from this common agent having any right to exclude a portion of the people, or "to make distinctions to their disadvantage," it is the duty of Congress to open the country by the removal of all obstructions, whether they be existing laws or anything else, and to give equal protection to all who may avail themselves of the right to use it. But you men of the North say that we of the South wish to carry our slaves there, and that the free labor of the North can not submit to the degradation of being associated with slave labor. Well, then we say, as the patriarch of old said to his friend and kinsman, when disputes arose between the herdsmen of their cattle: "Let there be no strife, I pray thee, between me and thee, and between my herdsmen and thy herdsmen, for we be brethren. Is not the whole land before thee? Separate thyself, I pray thee, from me. If thou wilt take the left hand, then I will go to the right; or, if thou depart to the right hand, then I will go to the left." In other words, we say, if you can not agree to enjoy this public domain in common, let us divide it. You take a share, and let us take a share. And I again submit to an intelligent and candid world if the proposition is not fair and just?—and whether its rejection does not amount to a clear expression of your fixed determination to exclude us entirely from any participation in this public domain?

Now, sir, all that we ask, or all that I ask, is for Congress to open the entire country, and give an equal right to all the citizens of all the States to enter, settle and colonize it with their property of every kind; or to make an equitable division of it. Is this wrong? Is it endeavoring to control the action of Congress improperly to carry out sectional views and interests? And am I to subject myself to the intended reproach of being an ultraist for insisting upon nothing but what is just and right? If so, I am willing to bear whatever of reproach the epithet may impart. If a man be an ultraist for insisting upon nothing but his rights, with a willingness to compromise even these upon any fair and reasonable terms, without a total abandonment, then I am an ultraist. And I am mistaken in the character of that people among whom I was born and with whom I have been reared, if a large majority of them, when all their propositions for adjustment and compromise shall have been rejected, will not be ultraists, too. Be not deceived and do not deceive others—this Union can never be maintained by force. With the confidence and affections of the people of all sections of the country, it is capable of being the strongest and best government on earth. But it can never be maintained upon any other principles than those upon which it was formed. All free governments are the creatures of volition—a breath can make them and a breath can destroy them. This government is no exception to the rule. And when once its spirit shall have departed, no power on earth can ever again infuse in it the Promethean spark of life and vitality. You might just as well attempt to raise the dead.

Mr. Chairman, when I look to the causes which lie at the bottom of these differences of opinion between the North and the South, and out of which this agitation springs; when I look at their character, extent, and radical nature— entering, as they necessarily do, into the very organization of society with us, I must confess that unpleasant apprehensions for the future permanent peace and quiet of the different States of this Union force themselves upon my mind. I am not, however, disposed to anticipate evil by indulging those apprehensions unless compelled to do so. It may be that we have the seeds of dissolution in our system which no skill can eradicate, just as we carry with us in our bodies the seeds of death which will certainly do their work at the allotted time. But because we are all conscious that we must die, it does not follow that we should hasten the event by an act of suicide. We have the business, duties, and obligations of life to discharge. So with this government. Because I may have serious apprehensions of the workings of causes known to exist, I do not conceive it therefore to be in the line of duty to anticipate the natural effects of those causes by any rash or unjustifiable act. I am disposed rather to hope for the best, while I feel bound to be prepared for the worst. What is really to be the future fate and destiny of this Republic is a matter of interesting speculation; but I am well satisfied that it can not last long, even if the present differences be adjusted, unless these violent and bitter sectional feelings of the North be kept out of the national halls. This is a conclusion that al must come to, who know anything of the lessons of history. But our business to-day is with the present, and not the future; and I would now invoke every member of this House who hears me, with the same frankness, earnestness, and singleness of purpose with which I have addressed them throughout these remarks, to come up like men and patriots, and relieve the country from the dangerous embarrassments by which it is at this time surrounded. It is a duty we owe to ourselves, to the millions we represent, and to the whole civilized world. To do this, I tell you again, there must be concessions by the North as well as the South. Are you not prepared to make them? Are feelings too narrow and restricted to embrace the whole country and to deal justly by all its parts? Have you formed a fixed, firm, and inflexible determination to carry your measures in this House by numerical strength, and then to enforce them by the bayonet? If so, you may be prepared to meet the consequences of whatever follows. The responsibility will rest upon your own heads. You may think that the suppression of an outbreak in the Southern States would be a holiday job for a few of your Northern regiments, but you may find to your cost, in the end, that seven millions of people fighting for their rights, their homes, and their hearthstones, can not be "easily conquered." I submit the matter to your deliberate consideration.

I have told you, sincerely and honestly, that I am for peace and the Union upon any fair and reasonable terms—it is the most cherished sentiment of my heart. But if you deny these terms—if you continue "deaf to the voice" of that spirit of justice, right, and equality, which should always characterize the deliberations of statesmen, I know of no other alternative that will be left to the people of the South, but, sooner or later, "to acquiesce in the necessity" of "holding you, as the rest of mankind, enemies in war—in peace, friends."

BRYANT

HIS WELCOME TO KOSSUTH[1]

(1851)

Born in 1794, died in 1878; admitted to the Bar in 1815; published "Thanatopsis" in 1816; became connected with the New York *Evening Post* in 1826, being Editor until his death; opposed the extension of slavery and supported the Union cause.

LET me ask you to imagine the contest, in which the United States asserted their independence of Great Britain, had been unsuccessful; that our armies, through treason or a league of tyrants against us, had been broken and scattered; that the great men who led them, and who swayed our councils—our Washington, our Franklin, and the venerable president of the American Congress—had been driven forth as exiles. If there had existed at that day, in any part of the civilized world, a powerful Republic, with institutions resting on the same foundations of liberty, which our own countrymen sought to establish, would there have been in that Republic any hospitality too cordial, any sympathy too deep, any zeal for their glorious but unfortunate cause, too fervent or too active to be shown toward these illustrious fugitives? Gentlemen, the case I have supposed is before

[1] Delivered at the banquet given by the Press of New York to Kossuth on December 15, 1851, Bryant presiding.

144

you. The Washingtons, the Franklins, the Hancocks of Hungary, driven out by a far worse tyranny than was ever endured here, are wanderers in foreign lands. Some of them have sought a refuge in our country—one sits with his company our guest to-night—and we must measure the duty we owe them by the same standard which we would have had history apply, if our ancestors had met with a fate like theirs.

I have compared the exiled Hungarians to the great men of our own history. Difficulty, my brethren, is the nurse of greatness—a harsh nurse, who roughly rocks her foster-children into strength and athletic proportion. The mind grappling with great aims and wrestling with mighty ingredients, grows, by certain necessity, to their stature. Scarce anything so convinces me of the capacity of the human intellect for indefinite expansion in the different stages of its being, as this power of enlarging itself to the compass of surrounding emergencies. These men have been trained to greatness by a quicker and surer method than a peaceful country and a tranquil period can know.

But it is not merely or principally for their personal qualities that we honor them; we honor them for the cause in which they failed so gloriously. Great issues hang upon that cause, and great interests of mankind are crushed by its downfall. I was on the continent of Europe when the treason of Görgey laid Hungary bound

at the feet of the Tsar. Europe was at that time
in the midst of the reaction; the ebb-tide was
rushing violently back, sweeping all that the
friends of freedom had planned into the black
bosom of the deep. In France the liberty of
the Press was extinct—Paris in a state of siege—
the soldiery of that Republic had just quenched
in blood the freedom of Rome—Austria had
suppressed liberty in northern Italy—absolutism
was restored in Russia, along the Rhine, and
in the towns and villages of Würtemberg and
Bavaria, troops withdrawn from the barracks
and garrisons filled the streets and kept the
inhabitants quiet with the bayonet at their
breast. Hungary at that moment alone upheld,
and upheld with a firm hand and dauntless
heart, the blazing torch of liberty. To Hungary
were turned the eyes, to Hungary clung the
hopes of all who did not despair of the freedom
of Europe.

I recollect that while the armies of Russia
were moving like a tempest from the North upon
the Hungarian host, the progress of events was
watched with the deepest solicitude by the people
of Germany. I was at that time in Munich, the
splendid capital of Bavaria. The Germans
seemed for the time to have put off their usual
character, and scrambled for the daily prints,
wet from the press, with such eagerness that
I almost thought myself in America. The news
of the catastrophe at last arrived; Görgey had
betrayed the cause of Hungary and yielded to

the demands of the Russians. Immediately a funeral gloom settled like a noonday darkness upon the city. I heard the muttered exclamations of the people, "It is all over—the last hope of European liberty is gone."

Russia did not misjudge. If she had allowed Hungary to become independent, or free, the reaction in favor of absolutism had been incomplete; there would have been one perilous example of successful resistance to despotism—in one corner of Europe a flame would have been kept alive, at which the other nations might have rekindled, among themselves, the light of liberty. Hungary was subdued; but does anyone who hears me believe that the present state of things in Europe will last? The despots themselves fear that it will not; and made cruel by their fears, are heaping chain on chain around the limbs of their subjects.

They are hastening the event they dread. Every added shackle galls, into a more fiery impotence, those who wear them. I look with mingling hope and horror to the day—a day bloodier, perhaps, than we have yet seen—when the exasperated nations shall snap their chains and start to their feet. It may well be that Hungary, made less patient of the yoke by the remembrance of her own many and glorious struggles for independence, and better fitted than other nations, by the peculiar structure of her institutions, for founding the liberty of her citizens on a rational basis, will take the lead. In that glorious and hazardous enterprise, in that hour of care, need, and peril, I hope she will be cheered and strengthened with aid from this side of the Atlantic; aid given not with the stinted hand, not with a cowardly and selfish apprehension, lest we should not err on the safe side—wisely, if you please. I care not with how broad a regard to the future, but in large, generous, effective measure.

And you, our guest, fearless, eloquent, large of heart and of mind, whose one thought is the salvation of oppressed Hungary, unfortunate but undiscouraged, struck down in the battle of liberty, but great in defeat, and gathering strength for future triumphs, receive this at our hands, that in this great attempt of man to repossess himself of the rights which God gave him, tho the strife be waged under a distant belt of longitude, and with the mightiest despotism of the world, the Press of America takes part with you and your countrymen. I give you—"LOUIS KOSSUTH."

RUFUS CHOATE

HIS EULOGY OF WEBSTER [1]

(1853)

Born in 1799, died in 1859; elected to Congress in 1830; reelected in 1832 and resigned in 1834; United States Senator in 1841, serving while Webster was Secretary of State; succeeded by Webster in 1845.

WEBSTER possessed the element of an impressive character, inspiring regard, trust, and admiration, not unmingled with love. It had, I think, intrinsically a charm such as belongs only to a good, noble, and beautiful nature. In its combination with so much fame, so much force of will, and so much intellect, it filled and fascinated the imagination and heart. It was affectionate in childhood and youth, and it was more than ever so in the few last months of his long life. It is the universal testimony that he gave to his parents, in largest measure, honor, love, obedience; that he eagerly appropriated the first means which he could command to relieve the father from the debts contracted to educate his brother and himself; that he selected his first place of professional practise that he might soothe the coming on of his old age.

[1] From a commemorative address before the faculty, students, and alumni of Dartmouth College on July 27, 1853. Choate, as well as Webster, was a graduate of Dartmouth.

Equally beautiful was his love of all his kindred and of all his friends. When I hear him accused of selfishness, and a cold, bad nature, I recall him lying sleepless all night, not without tears of boyhood, conferring with Ezekiel how the darling desire of both hearts should be compassed, and he, too, admitted to the precious privileges of education; courageously pleading the cause of both brothers in the morning; prevailing by the wise and discerning affection of the mother; suspending his studies of the law, and registering deeds and teaching school to earn the means, for both, of availing themselves of the opportunity which the parental self-sacrifice had placed within their reach; loving him through life, mourning him when dead, with a love and a sorrow very wonderful, passing the sorrow of woman; I recall the husband, the father of the living and of the early departed, the friend, the counselor of many years, and my heart grows too full and liquid for the refutation of words.

His affectionate nature, craving ever friendship, as well as the presence of kindred blood, diffused itself through all his private life, gave sincerity to all his hospitalities, kindness to his eye, warmth to the pressure of his hand, made his greatness and genius unbend themselves to the playfulness of childhood, flowed out in graceful memories indulged of the past or the dead, of incidents when life was young and promised to be happy,—gave generous sketches of his rivals,—the high contention now hidden by the handful of earth,—hours passed fifty years ago with great authors, recalled for the vernal emotions which then they made to live and revel in the soul. And from these conversations of friendship, no man—no man, old or young—went away to remember one word of profaneness, one allusion of indelicacy, one impure thought, one unbelieving suggestion, one doubt cast on the reality of virtue, of patriotism, of enthusiasm, of the progress of man,—one doubt cast on righteousness, or temperance, or judgment to come.

I have learned by evidence the most direct and satisfactory, that in the last months of his life, the whole affectionateness of his nature—his consideration of others; his gentleness; his desire to make them happy and to see them happy—seemed to come out in more and more beautiful and habitual expressions than ever before. The long day's public tasks were felt to be done; the cares, the uncertainties, the mental conflicts of high place, were ended; and he came home to recover himself for the few years which he might still expect would be his before he should go hence to be here no more. And there, I am assured and fully believe, no unbecoming regrets pursued him; no discontent, as for injustice suffered or expectations unfulfilled; no self-reproach for anything done or anything omitted by himself; no irritation, no peevishness unworthy of his noble nature; but instead, love and hope for his country, when she became the subject of conversation, and for all around him, the dearest and most indifferent, for all breathing things about him, the overflow of the kindest heart growing in gentleness and benevolence— paternal, patriarchal affections, seeming to become more natural, warm, and communicative every hour. Softer and yet brighter grew the tints on the sky of parting day; and the last lingering rays, more even than the glories of noon, announced how divine was the source from which they proceeded; how incapable to be quenched; how certain to rise on a morning which no night should follow.

Such a character was made to be loved. It was loved. Those who knew and saw it in its hour of calm—those who could repose on that soft green—loved him. His plain neighbors loved him; and one said, when he was laid in his grave, "How lonesome the world seems!" Educated young men loved him. The ministers of the gospel, the general intelligence of the country, the masses afar off, loved him. True, they had not found in his speeches, read by millions, so much adulation of the people; so much of the music which robs the public reason of itself; so many phrases of humanity and philanthropy; and some had told them he was lofty and cold—solitary in his greatness; but every year they came nearer and nearer to him, and as they came nearer, they loved him better; they heard how tender the son had been, the husband, the brother, the father, the friend, and neighbor; that he was plain, simple, natural, generous, hospitable—the heart larger than the brain; that he loved little children and reverenced God, the Scriptures, the Sabbath-day, the Constitution, and the law—and their hearts clave unto him. More truly of him than even of the great naval darling of England might it be said that "his presence would set the church-bells ringing, and give schoolboys a holiday,—would bring children from school and old men from the chimney-corner, to gaze on him ere he died." The great and unavailing lamentations first revealed the deep place he had in the hearts of his countrymen.

You are now to add to this his extraordinary power of influencing the convictions of others by speech, and you have completed the survey of the means of his greatness. And here, again, I begin, by admiring an aggregate made up of excellences and triumphs, ordinarily deemed incompatible. He spoke with consummate ability to the bench, and yet exactly as, according to every sound canon of taste and ethics, the bench ought to be addressed. He spoke with consummate ability to the jury, and yet exactly as, according to every sound canon, that totally different tribunal ought to be addressed. In the halls of Congress, before the people assembled for political discussion in masses, before audiences smaller and more select, assembled for some solemn commemoration of the past or of the dead,

—in each of these, again, his speech, of the first form of ability, was exactly adapted, also, to the critical proprieties of the place; each achieved, when delivered, the most instant and and specific success of eloquence—some of them in a splendid and remarkable degree; and yet, stranger still, when reduced to writing, as they fell from his lips, they compose a body of reading, in many volumes—solid, clear, rich, and full of harmony—a classical and permanent political literature.

And yet all these modes of his eloquence, exactly adapted each to its stage and its end, were stamped with his image and superscription, identified by characteristics incapable to be counterfeited and impossible to be mistaken. The same high power of reason, intent in every one to explore and display some truth; some truth of judicial, or historical, or biographical fact; some truth of law, deduced by construction, perhaps, or by illation; some truth of policy, for want whereof a nation, generations, may be the worse—reason seeking and unfolding truth; the same tone, in all, of deep earnestness, expressive of strong desire that that which he felt to be important should be accepted as true, and spring up to action; the same transparent, plain, forcible, and direct speech, conveying his exact thought to the mind—not something less or more; the same sovereignty of form, of brow, and eye, and tone, and manner—everywhere the intellectual king of men, standing before you—that same marvelousness of qualities and results, residing, I know not where, in words, in pictures, in the ordering of ideas, in felicities indescribable, by means whereof, coming from his tongue, all things seemed mended—truth seemed more true, probability more plausible, greatness more grand, goodness more awful, every affection more tender than when coming from other tongues—these are, in all, his eloquence.

But sometimes it became individualized and discriminated even from itself; sometimes place and circumstances, great interests at stake, a stage, an audience fitted for the highest historic action, a crisis, personal or national, upon him, stirred the depths of that emotional nature, as the anger of the goddess stirs the sea on which the great epic is beginning; strong passions, themselves kindled to intensity, quickened every faculty to a new life; the stimulated associations of ideas brought all treasures of thought and knowledge within command; the spell, which often held his imagination fast, dissolved, and she arose and gave him to choose of her urn of gold; earnestness became vehemence, the simple, perspicuous, measured, and direct language became a headlong, full, and burning tide of speech; the discourse of reason, wisdom, gravity, and beauty, changed to that superhuman, that rarest consummate eloquence—grand, rapid, pathetic, terrible; the *aliquid immensum infinitumque* that Cicero might have recognized; the master triumph of man in the rarest opportunity of his noblest power.

Such elevation above himself, in congressional debate, was most uncommon. Some such there were in the great discussions of executive power following the removal of the deposits, which they who heard them will never forget, and some which rest in the tradition of hearers only. But there were other fields of oratory on which, under the influence of more uncommon springs of inspiration, he exemplified, in still other forms, an eloquence in which I do not know that he has had a superior among men. Addressing masses by tens of thousands in the open air, on the urgent political question of the day, or designated to lead the meditations of an hour devoted to the remembrance of some national era, or of some incident marking the progress of the nation, and lifting him up to a view of what is, and what is past, and some indistinct revelation of the glory that lies in the future, or of some great historical name, just borne by the nation to his tomb—we have learned that then and there, at the base of Bunker Hill, before the corner-stone was laid, and again when from the finished column the centuries looked on him; in Faneuil Hall, mourning for those with whose spoken or written eloquence of freedom its arches had so often resounded; on the Rock of Plymouth; before the Capitol, of which there shall not be one stone left on another before his memory shall have ceased to live—in such scenes, un-fettered by the laws of forensic or parliamentary debate, multitudes uncounted lifting up their eyes to him; some great historical scenes of America around; all symbols of her glory and art and power and fortune there; voices of the past, not unheard; shapes beckoning from the future, not unseen—sometimes that mighty intellect, borne upward to a height and kindled to an illumination which we shall see no more, wrought out, as it were, in an instant a picture of vision, warning, prediction; the progress of the nation; the contrasts of its eras; the heroic deaths; the motives to patriotism; the maxims and arts imperial by which the glory has been gathered and may be heightened—wrought out, in an instant, a picture to fade only when all record of our mind shall die.

In looking over the public remains of his oratory, it is striking to remark how, even in that most sober and massive understanding and nature, you see gathered and expressed the characteristic sentiments and the passing time of our America. It is the strong old oak which ascends before you; yet our soil, our heaven, are attested in it as perfectly as if it were a flower that could grow in no other climate and in no other hour of the year or day. Let me instance in one thing only. It is a peculiarity of some schools of eloquence that they embody and utter, not merely the individual genius and character of the speaker, but a national consciousness—a national era, a mood, a hope, a dread, a despair—in which you listen to the spoken history of the time. There is an eloquence of an expiring nation, such as seems to sadden the glorious speech of Demosthenes; such as breathes grand and gloomy from the visions of the prophets of the last days of Israel and Judah; such as gave a spell to the expression of Grattan and of Kossuth—the sweetest, most mournful, most awful of the words which man may utter, or which man may hear—the eloquence of a perishing nation.

There is another eloquence, in which the national consciousness of a young or renewed and vast strength, of trust in a dazzling, certain, and limitless future, an inward glorying in victories yet to be won, sounds out as by voice of clarion, challenging to contest for the highest prize of earth; such as that in which the leader of Israel in its first days holds up to the new nation the Land of Promise; such as that which in the well-imagined speeches scattered by Livy over the history of the "majestic series of victories" speaks the Roman consciousness of growing aggrandizement which should subject the world; such as that through which, at the tribunes of her revolution, in the bulletins of her rising soldiers, France told to the world her dream of glory.

And of this kind somewhat is ours—cheerful, hopeful, trusting, as befits youth and spring; the eloquence of a State beginning to ascend to the first class of power, eminence, and consideration, and conscious of itself. It is to no purpose that they tell you it is in bad taste; that it partakes of arrogance and vanity; that a true national good breeding would not know, or seem to know, whether the nation is old or young; whether the tides of being are in their flow or ebb; whether these coursers of the sun are sinking slowly to rest, wearied with a journey of a thousand years, or just bounding from the Orient unbreathed. Higher laws than those of taste determine the consciousness of nations. Higher laws than those of taste determine the general forms of the expression of that consciousness. Let the downward age of America find its orators and poets and artists to erect its spirit, or grace and soothe its dying; be it ours to go up with Webster to the Rock, the Monument, the Capitol, and bid "the distant generations hail!"

Until the seventh day of March, 1850, I think it would have been accorded to him by an almost universal acclaim, as general and as expressive of profound and intelligent conviction and of enthusiasm, love, and trust, as ever saluted conspicuous statesmanship, tried by many crises of affairs in a great nation, agitated ever by parties, and wholly free.

SUMNER

ON THE CRIME AGAINST KANSAS [1]
(1856)

Born in 1811, died in 1874; admitted to the Bar in 1834; an unsuccessful Free Soil candidate for Congress in 1848; elected United States Senator by Free Soil and Democratic votes in 1851; assaulted in the Senate by Preston Brooks in 1856; reelected Senator as a Republican in 1857, 1863 and 1869; advocated the Civil Rights Bill for negroes; joined the Liberal Republican party in 1872.

You are now called to redress a great transgression. Seldom in the history of nations has such a question been presented. Tariffs, army bills, navy bills, land bills, are important, and justly occupy your care; but these all belong to the course of ordinary legislation. As means and instruments only, they are necessarily subordinate to the conservation of government itself. Grant them or deny them, in greater or

[1] Delivered in the United States Senate, May 15-20, 1856. It was this speech that led to the famous assault on Sumner by Preston S. Brooks. Sumner had severely arraigned Senator Butler of South Carolina, an uncle of Brooks, Brooks being himself a member of Congress from the same State. Two days after Sumner finished his speech, while he was sitting at his desk alone in the Senate-chamber, after the adjournment, Brooks entered and, after speaking a few words, struck Sumner violently on the head with a heavy stick. While Sumner was trying to extricate himself from his seat at the desk, Brooks repeated the blows until Sumner sank to the floor, bloody and senseless. Morefield Storey, one of Sumner's biographers, says Brooks's cane was "a heavy gutta-percha cane" and that the blows were continued "until the cane broke." So great was the excitement produced in the country by this event, that many pre-

less degree, and you will inflict no shock. The machinery of government will continue to move. The State will not cease to exist. Far otherwise is it with the eminent question now before you, involving, as it does, liberty in a broad territory, and also involving the peace of the whole country, with our good name in history for ever more.

Take down your map, sir, and you will find that the Territory of Kansas, more than any other region, occupies the middle spot of North America, equally distant from the Atlantic on the east, and the Pacific on the west; from the frozen waters of Hudson's Bay on the north, and the tepid Gulf Stream on the south, constituting the precise Territorial center of the whole vast continent. To such advantages of situation, on the very highway between two oceans, are added a soil of unsurpassed richness, and a fascinating, undulating beauty of surface, with a health-giving climate, calculated to nurture a

dicted that civil war would come at once. Sumner was long incapacitated for further work, remaining absent from the Senate nearly four years. An effort was made in the House to expel Brooks. He was censured, but the necessary two-thirds vote for expulsion could not be secured. Brooks then resigned (on July 14), but was reelected by his district in South Carolina, receiving all the votes cast except six, and on August 1 took his seat again.

The judgment of later times on Sumner's speech as an attack on Butler, has not been favorable to Sumner. Rhodes says: "The vituperation was unworthy of him and his cause, and the allusion to Butler's condition while speaking (Butler being absent from Washington at the time), ungenerous and pharisaical." Seward read the speech before its delivery, and in vain advised a toning down of the offensive remarks. Abridged.

powerful and generous people, worthy to be a central pivot of American institutions. A few short months only have passed since this spacious and mediterranean country was open only to the savage who ran wild in its woods and prairies; and now it has already drawn to its bosom a population of freemen larger than Athens crowded within her historic gates, when her sons, under Miltiades, won liberty for mankind on the field of Marathon; more than Sparta contained when she ruled Greece, and sent forth her devoted children, quickened by a mother's benediction, to return with their shields, or on them; more than Rome gathered on her seven hills, when, under her kings, she commenced that sovereign sway, which afterward embraced the whole earth; more than London held, when, on the fields of Crecy and Agincourt, the English banner was carried victoriously over the chivalrous hosts of France.

Against this Territory, thus fortunate in position and population, a crime has been committed, which is without example in the records of the past. Not in plundered provinces or in the cruelties of selfish governors will you find its parallel; and yet there is an ancient instance, which may show at least the path of justice. In the terrible inpeachment by which the great Roman orator has blasted through all time the name of Verres, amid charges of robbery and sacrilege, the enormity which most aroused the indignant voice of his accuser, and which still stands forth with strongest distinctness, arresting the sympathetic indignation of all who read the story, is, that away in Sicily he had scourged a citizen of Rome—that the cry, "I am a Roman citizen," had been interposed in vain against the lash of the tyrant governor. Other charges were that he had carried away productions of art, and that he had violated the sacred shrines. It was in the presence of the Roman Senate that this arraignment proceeded; in a temple of the Forum; amid crowds—such as no orator had ever before drawn together—thronging the porticos and colonnades, even clinging to the housetops and neighboring slopes—and under the anxious gaze of witnesses summoned from the scene of crime.

But an audience grander far—of higher dignity—of more various people, and of wider intelligence—the countless multitude of succeeding generations, in every land where eloquence has been studied, or where the Roman name has been recognized—has listened to the accusation, and throbbed with condemnation of the criminal. Sir, speaking in an age of light, and a land of constitutional liberty, where the safeguards of elections are justly placed among the highest triumphs of civilization, I fearlessly assert that the wrongs of much-abused Sicily, thus memorable in history, were small by the side of the wrongs of Kansas, where the very shrines of popular institutions, more sacred than any heathen altar, have been desecrated; where the ballot-box, more precious than any work, in ivory or marble, from the cunning hand of art, has been plundered; and where the cry, "I am an American citizen," has been interposed in vain against outrage of every kind, even upon life itself. Are you against sacrilege? I present it for your execration. Are you against robbery? I hold it up to your scorn. Are you for the protection of American citizens? I show you how their dearest rights have been cloven down, while a tyrannical usurpation has sought to instal itself on their very necks!

But the wickedness which I now begin to expose is immeasurably aggravated by the motive which prompted it. Not in any common lust for power did this uncommon tragedy have its origin. It is the rape of a virgin Territory, compelling it to the hateful embrace of slavery; and it may be clearly traced to a depraved longing for a new slave State, the hideous offspring of such a crime, in the hope of adding to the power of slavery in the national government. Yes, sir, when the whole world, alike Christian and Turk, is rising up to condemn this wrong, and to make it a hissing to the nations, here in our Republic, *force*—ay, sir, FORCE—has been openly employed in compelling Kansas to this pollution, and all for the sake of political power. There is the simple fact which you will in vain attempt to deny, but which in itself presents an essential wickedness that makes other public crimes seem like public virtues.

But this enormity, vast beyond comparison, swells to dimensions of wickedness which the imagination toils in vain to grasp, when it is understood that for this purpose are hazarded the horrors of intestine feud not only in this distant Territory, but everywhere throughout the country. Already the muster has begun. The strife is no longer local but national. Even now, while I speak, portents hang on all the arches of the horizon threatening to darken the broad land which already yawns with the mutterings of civil war; the fury of the propagandists of slavery, and the calm determination of their opponents, are now diffused from the distant Territory over widespread communities, and the whole country, in all its extent—marshaling hostile divisions, and foreshadowing a strife which, unless happily averted by the triumph of freedom, will become war—fratricidal, parricidal war—with an accumulated wickedness beyond the wickedness of any war in human annals, justly provoking the avenging judgment of providence and the avenging pen of history, and constituting a strife, in the language of the ancient writer, more than *foreign,* more than *social,* more than *civil;* but something compounded of all these strifes, and in itself more than war; *sed potius commune quoddam ex omnibus, et plus quam bellum.*

Such is the crime which you are to judge. But the criminal also must be dragged into day, that you may see and measure the power by which all this wrong is sustained. From no common source could it proceed. In its perpetration was needed a spirit of vaulting ambition which would hesitate at nothing; a hardihood of purpose which was insensible to the judgment of mankind; a madness for slavery which would disregard the Constitution, the laws, and all the great examples of our history; also a consciousness of power such as comes from the habit of power; a combination of energies found only in a hundred arms directed by a hundred eyes; a control of public opinion through venal pens and a prostituted Press; an ability to subsidize crowds in every vocation of life—the politician with his local importance, the lawyer with his subtle tongue, and even the authority of the judge on the bench; and a familiar use of men in places high and low, so that none, from the president to the lowest border postmaster, should decline to be its tool; all these things and more were needed, and they were found in the slave power of our Republic. There, sir, stands the criminal, all unmasked before you—heartless, grasping, and tyrannical—with an audacity beyond that of Verres, a subtlety beyond that of Machiavelli, a meanness beyond that of Bacon, and an ability beyond that of Hastings. Justice to Kansas can be secured only by the prostration of this influence; for this the power behind—greater than any president—which succors and sustains the crime.

Nay, the proceedings I now arraign derive their fearful consequences only from this connection.

In now opening this great matter, I am not insensible to the austere demands of the occasion; but the dependence of the crime against Kansas upon the slave power is so peculiar and important, that I trust to be pardoned while I impress it with an illustration which to some may seem trivial. It is related in Northern mythology that the god of Force, visiting an enchanted region, was challenged by his royal entertainer to what seemed a humble feat of strength—merely, sir, to lift a cat from the ground. The god smiled at the challenge, and calmly placing his hand under the belly of the animal with superhuman strength strove, while the back of the feline monster arched far upward, even beyond reach, and one paw actually forsook the earth, until at last the discomfited divinity desisted; but he was little surprised at his defeat when he learned that this creature, which seemed to be a cat and nothing more, was not merely a cat, but that it belonged to and was a part of the great Terrestrial Serpent, which, in its innumerable folds, encircled the whole globe. Even so the creature whose paws are now fastened upon Kansas, whatever it may seem to be, constitutes in reality a part of the slave power which, in its loathsome folds, is now coiled about the whole land. Thus do I expose the extent of the present contest, where we encounter not merely local resistance, but also the unconquered sustaining arm behind. But out of the vastness of the crime attempted, with all its woe and shame, I derive a well-founded assurance of a commensurate vastness of effort against it and by the aroused masses of the country, determined not only to vindicate right against wrong, but to redeem the Republic from the thraldom of that oligarchy which prompts, directs, and concentrates the distant wrong.

Such is the crime, and such is the criminal, which it is my duty in this debate to expose, and, by the blessing of God, this duty shall be done completely to the end.

The senator from South Carolina has read many books of chivalry, and believes himself a chivalrous knight with sentiments of honor and courage. Of course he has chosen a mistress to whom he has made his vows, and who, tho ugly to others, is always lovely to him; tho polluted in the sight of the world, is chaste in his sight—I mean the harlot, Slavery. For her, his tongue is always profuse in words. Let her be impeached in character, or any proposition made to shut her out from the extension of her wantonness, and no extravagance of manner or hardihood of assertion is then too great for this senator. The frenzy of Don Quixote in behalf of his wench, Dulcinea del Toboso, is all surpassed. The asserted rights of slavery, which shock equality of all kinds, are cloaked by a fantastic claim of equality. If the slave

States can not enjoy what, in mockery of the great fathers of the Republic, he misnames equality under the Constitution—in other words, the full power in the national Territories to compel fellow men to unpaid toil, to separate husband and wife, and to sell little children at the auction block—then, sir, the chivalric senator will conduct the State of South Carolina out of the Union! Heroic knight! Exalted senator! A second Moses come for a second exodus!

But not content with this poor menace, which we have been twice told was "measured," the senator, in the unrestrained chivalry of his nature, has undertaken to apply opprobrious words to those who differ from him on this floor. He calls them "sectional and fanatical"; and opposition to the usurpation in Kansas he denounces as "an uncalculating fanaticism." To be sure these charges lack all grace of originality, and all sentiment of truth; but the adventurous senator does not hesitate. He is the uncompromising, unblushing representative on this floor of a flagrant *sectionalism* which now domineers over the Republic, and yet with a ludicrous ignorance of his own position—unable to see himself as others see him—or with an effrontery which even his white head ought not to protect from rebuke, he applies to those here who resist his *sectionalism* the very epithet which designates himself. The men who strive to bring back the government to its original policy, when freedom and not slavery was sectional, he arraigns as *sectional*. This will not do. It involves too great a perversion of terms. I tell that senator that it is to himself and to the "organization" of which he is the "committed advocate," that this epithet belongs. I now fasten it upon them. For myself, I care little for names; but since the question has been raised here, I affirm that the Republican party of the Union is in no just sense *sectional*, but, more than any other party, *national;* and that it now goes forth to dislodge from the high places of the government the tyrannical sectionalism of which the senator from South Carolina is one of the maddest zealots.

With regret I come again upon the senator from South Carolina [Mr. Butler] who, omnipresent in this debate, overflowed with rage at the simple suggestion that Kansas had applied for admission as a State; and, with incoherent phrases, discharged the loose expectoration of his speech, now upon her representative, and then upon her people. There was no extravagance of the ancient parliamentary debate which he did not repeat; nor was there any possible deviation from truth which he did not make, with so much of passion, I am glad to add, as to save him from the suspicion of intentional aberration. But the senator touches nothing which he does not disfigure with error—sometimes of principle, sometimes of fact. He shows an incapacity of accuracy whether in stating the Constitution or in stating the law; whether in the details of statistics or the diversions of scholarship. He can not open his mouth but out there flies a blunder. Surely he ought to be familiar with the life of Franklin; and yet he referred to this household character, while acting as agent of our fathers in England, as above suspicion; and this was done that he might give point to a false contrast with the agent of Kansas—not knowing that, however they may differ in genius and fame, in this experience they are alike: that Franklin, when intrusted with the petition of Massachusetts Bay, was assaulted by a foul-mouthed speaker, where he could not be heard in defense, and denounced as a "thief," even as the agent of Kansas has been assaulted on this floor and denounced as a "forger." And let not the vanity of the senator be inspired by the parallel with the British statesman of that day; for it is only in hostility to freedom that any parallel can be recognized.

But it is against the people of Kansas that the sensibilities of the senator are particularly aroused. Coming, as he announces, "from a State"—ay, sir, from South Carolina—he turns with lordly disgust from this newly-formed community, which he will not recognize even as a "body politic." Pray, sir, by what title does he indulge in this egotism? Has he read the history of "the State" which he represents? He can not surely have forgotten its shameful imbecility from slavery, confessed throughout the Revolution, followed by its more shameful assumptions for slavery since. He can not have forgotten its wretched persistence in the slave trade as the very apple of its eye, and the condition of its participation in the Union. He can not have forgotten its Constitution, which is Republican only in name, confirming power in the hands of the few, and founding the qualifications of its legislators on "a settled freehold estate and ten negroes."

And yet the senator, to whom that "State" has in part committed the guardianship of its good name, instead of moving with backward treading steps, to cover its nakedness, rushes forward in the very ecstacy of madness, to expose it by provoking a comparison with Kansas. South Carolina is old; Kansas is young. South Carolina counts by centuries, where Kansas counts by years. But a beneficent example may be born in a day; and I venture to say that against the two centuries of the older "State" may be already set the two years of trial, evolving corresponding virtue, in the younger community. In the one is the long wail of slavery; in the other, the hymns of freedom. And if we glance at special achievements, it will be difficult to find anything in the history of South Carolina which presents so much of heroic spirit in an heroic cause as appears in that repulse of the Missouri invaders by the be-

leaguered town of Lawrence, where even the
women gave their effective efforts to freedom.

The matrons of Rome, who poured their jewels
into the Treasury for the public defense—the
wives of Prussia who, with delicate fingers,
clothed their defenders against French invasion
—the mothers of our own Revolution, who sent
forth their sons, covered with prayers and
blessings, to combat for human rights, did
nothing of self-sacrifice truer than did these
women on this occasion. Were the whole history
of South Carolina blotted out of existence
from its very beginning down to the day of the
last election of the senator to his present seat
on this floor, civilization might lose—I do not
say how little, but surely less than it has already
gained by the example of Kansas in its valiant
struggle against oppression, and in the development of a new science of emigration. Already,
in Lawrence alone, there are newspapers and
schools, including a high school, and throughout this infant Territory there is more mature
scholarship far, in proportion to its inhabitants,
than in all South Carolina. Ah, sir, I tell the
senator that Kansas, welcomed as a free State,
will be a "ministering angel" to the Republic
when South Carolina, in the cloak of darkness
which she hugs, "lies howling."

PRESTON S. BROOKS

IN DEFENSE OF HIS ATTACK ON SUMNER [1]
(1856)

Born in 1819, died in 1857; elected to Congress from South Carolina in 1853, serving until 1856, when, after the failure of the attempt to expel him, he resigned and appealed to his constituents, who reelected him in the same year almost without opposition; served until his death on January 27, 1857.

SOME time since a senator from Massachusetts allowed himself, in an elaborately prepared speech, to offer a gross insult to my State, and to a venerable friend who is my State representative and who was absent at the time. Not content with that, he published to the world, and circulated extensively, this uncalled-for libel on my State and my blood. Whatever insults my State insults me. Her history and character have commanded my pious veneration; and in her defense I hope I shall always be prepared, humbly and modestly, to perform the duty of a son. I should have forfeited my own self-respect, and perhaps the good opinion of my countrymen, if I had failed to resent such an injury by calling the offender in question to a personal account. It was a personal affair, and in taking redress into my own hands I meant

[1] Delivered in the House of Representatives on July 14, 1856. Abridged. The assault occurred on May 22.

no disrespect to the Senate of the United States or to this House.

But if I had committed a breach of privilege, it was the privilege of the Senate, and not of this House, which was violated. I was answerable *there* and not *here*. They had no right, as it seems to me, to prosecute me in these Halls; nor have you the right in law or under the Constitution, as I respectfully submit, to take jurisdiction over offenses committed against them. The Constitution does not justify them in making such a request, nor this House in granting it. If, unhappily, the day should ever come when sectional or party feeling should run so high as to control all other considerations of public duty or justice, how easy it will be to use such precedents for the excuse of arbitrary power, in either House, to expel members of the minority who may have rendered themselves obnoxious to the prevailing spirit in the House to which they belong.

If I desired to kill the senator why did I not do it? You all admit that I had him in my power. It was expressly to avoid taking life that I used an ordinary cane, presented to me by a friend in Baltimore nearly three months before its application to the "bare head" of the Massachusetts senator. I went to work very deliberately, as I am charged—and this is admitted—and speculated somewhat as to whether I should employ a horsewhip or a cowhide; but knowing that the senator was my superior in strength, it occurred to me that he might wrest it from my hand, and then—for I never attempt anything I do not perform—I might have been compelled to do that which I would have regretted the balance of my natural life.

My answer is, that the senator would not accept a message; and having formed the unalterable determination to punish him, I believed that the offense of "sending a hostile message," superadded to the indictment for assault and battery, would subject me to legal penalties more severe than would be imposed for a simple assault and battery. That is my answer.

To such as have given their votes and made their speeches on the constitutional principles involved, and without indulging in personal vilification, I owe my respect. But, sir, they have written me down upon the history of the country as worthy of expulsion, and in no unkindness I must tell them that for all future time my self-respect requires that I shall pass them as strangers. And now, Mr. Speaker, I announce to you and to this House, that I am no longer a member of the Thirty-fourth Congress.[1]

[1] On concluding this speech Mr. Brooks walked out of the House.

SEWARD

HIS "IRREPRESSIBLE CONFLICT" SPEECH [1]

(1858)

Born in 1801, died in 1872; elected to the New York State Senate in
1830; an unsuccessful candidate for Governor of New York in 1834;
Governor of New York in 1838 and again in 1840; United States
Senator in 1849-61; prominent candidate for the Republican nomination for President in 1860; Secretary of State in 1861-69; his assas-
sination attempted at the time Lincoln was killed in 1865, being
severely wounded; prevailed on France to withdraw troops from
Mexico; negotiated the purchase of Alaska from Russia in 1867.

THE unmistakable outbreaks of zeal which
occur all around me show that you are earnest
men—and such a man am I. Let us, therefore,
at least for a time, pass all secondary and col-
lateral questions, whether of a personal or of
a general nature, and consider the main subject of the present canvass.

Our country is a theater which exhibits in
full operation two radically different political

[1] From a speech delivered from the stump in Rochester on October 25, 1858, and widely read and commented on at the time. Seward
was then the chief leader of the Republican party, and was regarded as its probable candidate for president in the election of
1860. Rhodes doubts if, in the position taken in this speech, Seward
was influenced by what Lincoln had said of similar import on June
17 of the same year, at Springfield. " He would at that time," says
Rhodes, "have certainly scorned the notion of borrowing ideas from
Lincoln; and had he studied the progress of the Illinois canvass, he
must have seen that the declaration did not meet with general
favor."

systems—the one resting on the basis of servile or slave labor, the other on the basis of voluntary labor of freemen.

The laborers who are enslaved are all negroes, or persons more or less purely of African derivation. But this is only accidental. The principle of the system is that labor in every society, by whomsoever performed, is necessarily unintellectual, groveling, and base; and that the laborer, equally for his own good and for the welfare of the State, ought to be enslaved. The white laboring man, whether native or foreigner, is not enslaved only because he can not as yet be reduced to bondage.

You need not be told now that the slave system is the older of the two and that once it was universal. The emancipation of our own ancestors, Caucasians and Europeans as they were, hardly dates beyond a period of five hundred years. The great melioration of human society which modern times exhibit is mainly due to the incomplete substitution of the system of voluntary labor for the old one of servile labor which has already taken place. This African slave system is one which, in its origin and its growth, has been altogether foreign from the habits of the races which colonized these States and established civilization here. It was introduced on this new continent as an engine of conquest and for the establishment of monarchical power by the Portuguese and the Spaniards, and was rapidly extended by them all over South

America, Central America, Louisiana, and Mexico. Its legitimate fruits are seen in the poverty, imbecility, and anarchy which now pervade all Portuguese and Spanish America.

The free-labor system is of German extraction, and it was established in our country by emigrants from Sweden, Holland, Germany, Great Britain, and Ireland. We justly ascribe to its influences the strength, wealth, greatness, intelligence, and freedom which the whole American people now enjoy. One of the chief elements of the value of human life is freedom in the pursuit of happiness. The slave system is not only intolerable, unjust, and inhuman toward the laborer, whom, only because he is a laborer, it loads down with chains and converts into merchandise; but is scarcely less severe upon the freeman, to whom, only because he is a laborer from necessity, it denies facilities for employment and whom it expels from the community because it can not enslave and convert him into merchandise also. It is necessarily improvident and ruinous because, as a general truth, communities prosper and flourish, or droop and decline in just the degree that they practise or neglect to practise the primary duties of justice and humanity. The free-labor system conforms to the divine law of equality which is written in the hearts and consciences of men, and therefore is always and everywhere beneficent.

The slave system is one of constant danger, distrust, suspicion and watchfulness. It debases those whose toil alone can produce wealth and resources for defense to the lowest degree of which human nature is capable—to guard against mutiny and insurrection; and thus wastes energies which otherwise might be employed in national development and aggrandizement.

Russia yet maintains slavery and is a despotism. Most of the other European States have abolished slavery and adopted the system of free labor. It was the antagonistic political tendencies of the two systems which the first Napoleon was contemplating when he predicted that Europe would ultimately be either all Cossack or all republican. Never did human sagacity utter a more pregnant truth. The two systems are at once perceived to be incongruous. But they are more than incongruous—they are incompatible. They never have permanently existed together in one country and they never can. It would be easy to demonstrate this impossibility from the irreconcilable contrast between their great principles and characteristics. But the experience of mankind has conclusively established it.

Slavery, as I have already intimated, existed in every State in Europe. Free labor has supplanted it everywhere except in Russia and Turkey. State necessities developed in modern times are now obliging even those two nations to encourage and employ free labor; and already, despotic as they are, we find them engaged in abolishing slavery. In the United States slavery came into collision with free labor at the close of the last century, and fell before it in New England, New York, New Jersey, and Pennsylvania, but triumphed over it effectually and excluded it for a period yet undetermined, from Virginia, the Carolinas, and Georgia. Indeed, so incompatible are the two systems that every new State which is organized within our ever-extending domain makes its first political act a choice of the one and the exclusion of the other, even at the cost of civil war if necessary. The slave States, without law, at the last national election successfully forbade, within their own limits, even the casting of votes for a candidate for president of the United States supposed to be favorable to the establishment of the free-labor system in new States.

Hitherto the two systems have existed in different States, but side by side within the American Union. This has happened because the Union is a confederation of States. But in another aspect the United States constitute only one nation. Increase of population, which is filling the States out to their very borders, together with a new and extended network of railroads and other avenues, and an internal commerce which daily becomes more intimate, is rapidly bringing the States into a higher and more perfect social unity or consolidation. Thus these antagonistic systems are continually coming into closer contact and collision results.

Shall I tell you what this collision means? They who think that it is accidental, unnecessary, the work of interested or fanatical agitators, and therefore ephemeral, mistake the case altogether. It is an irrepressible conflict between opposing and enduring forces, and it means that the United States must and will, sooner or later, become either entirely a slave-holding nation or entirely a free-labor nation. Either the cotton and rice-fields of South Carolina and the sugar plantations of Louisiana will ultimately be tilled by free labor, and Charleston and New Orleans become marts for legitimate merchandise alone, or else the rye-fields and wheat-fields of Massachusetts and New York must again be surrendered by their farmers to slave culture and to the production of slaves, and Boston and New York become once more markets for trade in the bodies and souls of men.

It is the failure to apprehend this great truth that induces so many unsuccessful attempts at final compromise between the slave and free States, and it is the existence of this great fact that renders all such pretended compromises, when made, vain and ephemeral. Startling as this saying may appear to you, fellow citizens, it is by no means an original or even a modern one. Our forefathers knew it to be true, and unanimously acted upon it when they framed the Constitution of the United States. They regarded the existence of the servile system in so many of the States with sorrow and shame, which they openly confessed, and they looked upon the collision between them, which was then just revealing itself, and which we are now accustomed to deplore, with favor and hope. They knew that either the one or the other system must exclusively prevail.

Unlike too many of those who in modern time invoke their authority, they had a choice between the two. They preferred the system of free labor, and they determined to organize the government and so to direct its activity that that system should surely and certainly prevail. For this purpose, and no other, they based the whole structure of government broadly on the principle that all men are created equal, and therefore free—little dreaming that within the short period of one hundred years their descendants would bear to be told by any orator, however popular, that the utterance of that principle was merely a rhetorical rhapsody; or by any judge, however venerated, that it was attended by mental reservations which rendered it hypocritical and false. By the Ordinance of 1787 they dedicated all of the national domain not yet polluted by slavery to free labor immediately, thenceforth and for ever; while by the new Constitution and laws they invited foreign free labor from all lands under the sun, and interdicted the importation of African slave labor, at all times, in all places, and under all circumstances whatsoever. It is true that they necessarily and wisely modified this policy of freedom by leaving it to the several States, affected as they were by differing circumstances, to abolish slavery in their own way and at their own pleasure, instead of confiding that duty to Congress; and that they secured to the slave States, while yet retaining the system of slavery, a three-fifths representation of slaves in the federal government, until they should find themselves able to relinquish it with safety. But the very nature of these modifications fortifies my position—that the fathers knew that the two systems could not endure within the Union, and expected that within a short period slavery would disappear for ever. Moreover, in order that these modifications might not altogether defeat their grand design of a republic maintaining universal equality, they provided that two-thirds of the States might amend the Constitution.

The very Constitution of the Democratic party commits it to execute all the designs of the slave-holders, whatever they may be. It is not a party of the whole Union—of all the free States and of all the slave States; nor yet is it a party of the free States in the North and in the Northwest; but it is a sectional and local party, having practically its seat within the slave States and counting its constituency chiefly and almost exclusively there. Of all its representatives in Congress and in the electoral colleges, two-thirds uniformly come from these States. Its great element of strength lies in the vote of the slave-holders, augmented by the representation of three-fifths of the slaves. Deprive the Democratic party of this strength and it would be a helpless and hopeless minority, incapable of continued organization. The Democratic party, being thus local and sectional, acquires new strength from the admission of every new slave State and loses relatively by the admission of every new free State into the Union.

JOHN BROWN

HIS SPEECH TO THE COURT AT HIS TRIAL [1]
(1859)

Born in 1800, died in 1859; removed to Kansas in 1855 in order to oppose the extension of slavery; gained a victory over an invading party from Missouri at Ossawatomie in August, 1856; seized the arsenal at Harper's Ferry, October, 1859, for the purpose of arming the negroes for an insurrection; captured two days later, tried by the Commonwealth of Virginia and executed.

I HAVE, may it please the court, a few words to say. In the first place, I deny everything but what I have all along admitted—the design on my part to free the slaves. I intended certainly to have made a clean thing of that matter, as I did last winter when I went into Missouri and there took slaves without the snapping of a gun on either side, moved them through the country, and finally left them in Canada. I designed to have done the same thing again on a larger scale. That was all I intended. I never did intend murder, or treason, or the destruction of

[1] His last speech to the court (November 2, 1859) before which he was tried at Charlestown, West Virginia, his execution taking place on December 2 of the same year. During the night before the execution a company of soldiers, with their arms and accouterments, slept in the court-room where Brown had been tried, and it is a curious fact that one of these soldiers was John Wilkes Booth.

186

property, or to excite or incite slaves to rebellion, or to make insurrection.

I have another objection; and that is, it is unjust that I should suffer such a penalty. Had I interfered in the manner which I admit, and which I admit has been fairly proved (for I admire the truthfulness and candor of the greater portion of the witnesses who have testified in this case)—had I so interfered in behalf of the rich, the powerful, the intelligent, the so-called great, or in behalf of any of their friends —either father, mother, brother, sister, wife, or children, or any of that class—and suffered and sacrificed what I have in this interference, it would have been all right; and every man in this court would have deemed it an act worthy of reward rather than punishment.

This court acknowledges, as I suppose, the validity of the law of God. I see a book kissed here which I suppose to be the Bible, or at least the New Testament. That teaches me that all things whatsoever I would that men should do to me, I should do even so to them. It teaches me, further, to "remember them that are in bonds, as bound with them." I endeavored to act up to that instruction. I say I am yet too young to understand that God is any respecter of persons. I believe that to have interfered as I have done— as I have always freely admitted I have done —in behalf of His despised poor was not wrong, but right. Now, if it is deemed necessary that I should forfeit my life for the furtherance of the ends of justice, and mingle my blood further with the blood of my children and with the blood of millions in this slave country whose rights are disregarded by wicked, cruel, and unjust enactments—I submit; so let it be done!

Let me say one word further.

I feel entirely satisfied with the treatment I have received on my trial. Considering all the circumstances it has been more generous than I expected. But I feel no consciousness of guilt. I have stated from the first what was my intention and what was not. I never had any design against the life of any person, nor any disposition to commit treason, or excite slaves to rebel, or make any general insurrection. I never encouraged any man to do so, but always discouraged any idea of that kind.

Let me say also a word in regard to the statements made by some of those connected with me. I hear it has been stated by some of them that I have induced them to join me. But the contrary is true. I do not say this to injure them, but as regretting their weakness. There is not one of them but joined me of his own accord, and the greater part of them at their own expense. A number of them I never saw, and never had a word of conversation with till the day they came to me; and that was for the purpose I have stated.

Now I have done.

GARRISON

ON THE DEATH OF JOHN BROWN [1]
(1859)

Born in 1805, died in 1879; began to publish *The Liberator* in 1831;
founded an Abolition Society in Boston in 1832; President of the
American Antislavery Society in 1843–65.

GOD forbid that we should any longer continue the accomplices of thieves and robbers, of
men-stealers and women-whippers! We must
join in the name of freedom. As for the Union
—where is it and what is it? In one-half of it
no man can exercise freedom of speech or the
Press—no man can utter the words of Washington, of Jefferson, of Patrick Henry—except at
the peril of his life; and Northern men are everywhere hunted and driven from the South, if
they are supposed to cherish the sentiment of
freedom in their bosoms. We are living under
an awful despotism—that of a brutal slave
oligarchy. And they threaten to leave us, if
we do not continue to do their work, as we have
hitherto done it, and go down in the dust before
them! Would to heaven they would go! It
would only be the paupers clearing out from
the town, would it not? But no, they do not

---

[1] Delivered in Boston a few weeks after John Brown was hanged
at Charlestown, West Virginia.

mean to go; they mean to cling to you and they mean to subdue you.

But will you be subdued? I tell you our work is the dissolution of this slavery-cursed Union, if we would have a fragment of our liberties left to us! Surely between freemen, who believe in exact justice and impartial liberty, and slave-holders, who are for cleaving down all human rights at a blow, it is not possible there should be any union whatever. "How can two walk together except they be agreed?" The slave-holder with his hands dripping in blood—will I make a compact with him? The man who plunders cradles—will I say to him: "Brother, let us walk together in unity?" The man who, to gratify his lust or his anger, scourges woman with the lash till the soil is red with her blood—will I say to him: "Give me your hand; let us form a glorious Union?" No, never—never! There can be no union between us. "What concord hath Christ with Belial?" What union has freedom with slavery? Let us tell the inexorable and remorseless tyrants of the South that their conditions hitherto imposed upon us, whereby we are morally responsible for the existence of slavery, are horribly inhuman and wicked, and we can not carry them out for the sake of their evil company.

By the dissolution of the Union we shall give the finishing blow to the slave system; and then God will make it possible for us to form a true, vital, enduring, all-embracing Union from the Atlantic to the Pacific—one God to be worshiped, one Savior to be revered, one policy to be carried out—freedom everywhere to all the people without regard to complexion or race— and the blessing of God resting upon us all! I want to see that glorious day! Now the South is full of tribulation and terror and despair, going down to irretrievable bankruptcy, and fearing each bush an officer! Would to God it might all pass away like a hideous dream! And how easily it might be! What is it that God requires of the South, to remove every root of bitterness, to allay every fear, to fill her borders with prosperity? But one simple act of justice, without violence and convulsion, without danger and hazard. It is this: "Undo the heavy burdens, break every yoke, and let the oppressed go free!"

How simple and how glorious! It is the complete solution of all the difficulties in the case. Oh that the South may be wise before it is too late, and give heed to the word of the Lord! But whether she will hear or forbear, let us renew our pledges to the cause of bleeding humanity, and spare no effort to make this truly the land of the free and the refuge of the oppressed!

> "Onward, then, ye fearless band,
> Heart to heart, and hand to hand;
> Yours shall be the Christian stand,
> Or the martyr's grave."

YANCEY

HIS SPEECH OF PROTEST IN THE CHARLESTON CONVENTION [1]

(1860)

Born in 1814, died in 1863; after being active against Nullification in
South Carolina, he removed to Alabama in 1836; prominent as an
Antiwhig orator in the Presidential campaign of 1840; elected to
Congress in 1844; fought a bloodless duel with Congressman Cling-
man in 1845; author of the "Alabama Platform" of 1847; vigor-
ously opposed the Clay Compromise of 1850; became famous as a
secession orator before the Civil War; led the seceders from the
Charleston Convention in 1860; went to Europe seeking recognition
from England and France of the Southern Confederacy; thereafter
until his death a member of the Confederate Senate.

IT has been charged, in order to demoralize
whatever influence we might be entitled to, either
from our personal or political characteristics or
as representatives of the State of Alabama, that
we are disruptionists, disunionists *per se;* that we
desire to break up the party in the State of Alabama, to break up the party in the Union, and to

[1] From his speech in the National Democratic Convention at
Charleston, April 28, 1860, in support of the protest of the Alabama
delegation. Printed here from a rare pamphlet report of the proceedings of the convention, found in the New York Public Library.
Yancey in this convention was the leader of the seceders, who
afterward met in Baltimore and nominated Breckenridge. Wood-
row Wilson says of Yancey's work at this time:

"It was he more than any other, who taught the South what
Douglas really meant; he more than any other, who split the ranks
of the Democratic party at Charleston, made the election of Douglas impossible, and brought Lincoln in."

dissolve the Union itself. Each and all of these allegations, come from what quarter they may, I pronounce to be false. There is no disunionist, that I know of, in the delegation from the State of Alabama. There is no disruptionist that I know of, and if there are factionists in our delegation they could not have got in there with the knowledge upon the part of our State Convention that they were of so unenviable a character.

We have come here, with the twofold purpose of saving the country and of saving the Democracy; and if the Democracy will not lend itself to that high, holy and elevated purpose; if it can not elevate itself above the mere question of how perfect shall be its mere personal organization and how widespread shall be its mere voting success, then we say to you, gentlemen, mournfully and regretfully, that, in the opinion of the State of Alabama, and I believe, of the whole South, you have failed in your mission, and it will be our duty to go forth and make an appeal to the loyalty of the country to stand by that Constitution which party organizations have deliberately rejected.

The South is in a minority, we have been tauntingly told to-day. In the progress of events and the march of civilization and emigration, the Northwest has grown up, from a mere infant in swaddling clothes, at the formation of the Constitution, into the form and proportions of a giant people; and owing to its institutions and demand for white labor, and the peculiar nature of our institutions, tho advancing side by side with us in parallel lines, but never necessarily in conflict, it has surpassed us greatly in numbers. We are, therefore, in a numerical minority. But we do not murmur at this; we cheerfully accept the result; but we as firmly claim the right of the minority—and what is that? We claim the benefit of the Constitution that was made for the protection of minorities.

In the march of events, feeling conscious of your numerical power, you have aggressed upon us. We hold up between us and your advancing columns of numbers that written instrument which your and our fathers made, and by the compact of which, you with your power were to respect as to us and our rights. Our and your fathers made it that they and their children should for ever observe it; that, upon all questions affecting the rights of the minority, the majority should not rely upon their voting numbers, but should look, in restraint upon passion, avarice and lust for power, to the written compact, to see in what the minority was to be respected, and how it was to be protected, and to yield an implicit obedience to that compact. Constitutions are made solely for the protection of the minorities in government, and for the guidance of majorities.

Ours are now the institutions which are at stake; ours is the peace that is to be destroyed; ours is the property that is to be destroyed; ours is the honor at stake—the honor of children, the honor of families, the lives, perhaps, of all of us. It all rests upon what your course may ultimately make out of a great heaving volcano of passion. Bear with us then, while we stand sternly upon what is yet a dormant volcano, and say that we can yield no position until we are convinced that we are wrong. We are in a position to ask you to yield. What right of yours, gentlemen of the North, have we of the South ever invaded? What institution of yours have we ever assailed, directly or indirectly? What laws have we ever passed that have invaded, or induced others to invade, the sanctity of your homes, or to put your lives in jeopardy, or that were likely to destroy the fundamental institutions of your States? The wisest, the most learned and the best among you remain silent, because you can not say that we have done this thing.

If your view is right and ours is not one strictly supported by the compact, still the consequence, in a remote degree, of your proposition, may bring a dreaded result upon us all. If you have no domestic, no municipal peace at stake, and no property at stake, and no fundamental institutions of your liberties at stake, are we asking any too much of you to-day when we ask you to yield to us in this matter as brothers, in order to quiet our doubts? For in yielding you lose nothing that is essentially right. Do I state that proposition, gentlemen, any stronger than your own intellects and your own judgment will thoroughly endorse? If I do, I am unconscious of it.

Turn the pages of the recent past as regards the possessions acquired in the Mexican War, in which, gentlemen, it is but modestly stating the fact when I say that Southern chivalry was equal to Northern chivalry—that Southern blood was poured out in equal quantities with Northern blood—and Southern genius shone as bright upon the battle-field as Northern genius; and yet, when the battle was done, and the glittering spoil was brought forward, a vast and disproportionate quantity was given to the North, while the South was made to take the portion of an almost portionless son.

In the Northern States the Democratic party was once overwhelmingly in the ascendent. Why are they not so now? And why is the South more unitedly Democratic? The answer is ready. Antislavery sentiment is dominant in the North—slavery sentiment is dominant in the South. And, gentlemen, let me tell you, if it is not presumption in me to tell you, why you have grown weaker and weaker. It is my belief, from some observation and reflection upon this subject, that you are not now in the ascendent in the North, because you have tampered with the antislavery feeling of that section. I do not mean that you have tampered with it, or yielded to it, as a matter of choice. I do not mean that you are wilful traitors to your convictions of duty; but this is what I do mean: Finding an overwhelming preponderance of power in that antislavery sentiment, believing it to be the common will of your people, you hesitated before it; you trembled at its march. You did not triumph over the young Hercules in his cradle, because you made no direct effort to do so.

There is a conviction in our minds that we can not be safe in the Union, unless we obtain your unequivocal pledge to an administration of this government upon plainly avowed constitutional, congressional, as well as executive and judicial, protection of our rights. You have objected that this is a new feature in Democracy. But I say you have taken jurisdiction of this question in years past. In 1844 you took jurisdiction of the slavery question, to protect it from assaults. In 1848 you again took jurisdiction of the slavery question, tho to a limited extent. In 1852 you did the same; and in 1856 when the Territorial issues were forced upon the country by the Freesoilers, you demanded that the Democratic party should take one step farther in advance, in order to be up with the progress of the times, and with the march of aggression. You then added to these former platforms another plank, which it was then deemed would be sufficient to meet the issues urged.

And what was that plank? It was that Congress should not intervene to establish or abolish slavery in State or Territory. What is the fair and just meaning of this proposition? Lawyers and statesmen who are in the habit of construing laws and constitutions by the light of experience and by the rules which the great jurists of all ages have laid down for their construction, know that in order to decide what a law of doubtful import means, you must look at the subject matter, at the cause of its enactment; you must look at the evils it was designed to correct, and the remedy it was designed to give.

Gentlemen of the Convention, that venerable, that able, that revered jurist, the honorable chief justice of the United States, trembling upon the very verge of the grave, for years kept merely alive by the pure spirit of patriotic duty that burns within his breast—a spirit that will not permit him to succumb to the gnawings of disease and to the weaknesses of mortality—which hold him, as it were, suspended between two worlds, with his spotless ermine around him, standing upon the very altar of justice, has given to us the utterance of the Supreme Court of the United States upon this very question.

Let the murmur of the hustings be stilled—let the voices of individual citizens, no matter how great and respected in their appropriate spheres, be hushed, while the law, as expounded by the constituted authority of the country, emotionless, passionless and just, rolls in its silvery cadence over the entire realm, from the Atlantic to the Pacific, and from the ice-bound regions of the North to the glittering waters of the Gulf. What says that decision? That decision tells you, gentlemen, that the Territorial Legislature has no power to interfere with the rights of the slave-owner in the Territory while in a Territorial condition. That decision tells you that this government is a union of sovereign States; which States are coequal, and in trust for which coequal States the government holds the Territories. It tells you that the people of those coequal States have a right to go into these Territories, thus held in trust, with every species of property which is recognized as property by the States in which they live, or by the Constitution of the United States.

But, we are met right here with this assertion: we are told by the distinguished advocate of this doctrine of popular sovereignty that this opinion is not a decision of the Supreme Court, but merely the opinion of citizen Taney. He does not tell you, my countrymen, that it is not the opinion of the great majority of the Supreme Court bench. Oh, no! but he tells you that it is a matter that is *obiter dicta,* outside the jurisdiction of the Court; in other words, extra-judicial—that it is simply the opinion of Chief Justice Taney, as an individual, and not the decision of the Court because it was not the subject-matter before the Court.

Now, Mr. Douglas and all others who make that assertion and undertake to get rid of the moral, the constitutional, the intellectual power of the argument, put themselves directly in conflict with the venerable chief justice of the

Supreme Court of the United States, and with the recorded decision of the Court itself; because Chief Justice Taney, after disposing of the demurrer in that case, undertook to go on and to decide the question upon the facts and the merits of the case; and, said he, in doing that we are met with the objection, "That anything we may say upon that part of the case will be extra-judicial and mere *obiter dicta*. This is a manifest mistake," etc.; and the Court—not Chief Justice Taney, but the whole Court, with but two dissenting voices—decided that it was not *obiter dicta*; that it was exactly in point, within the jurisdiction of the Court, and that it was the duty of the Court to decide it.

Now then, who shall the Democracy recognize as authority on this point—a statesman, no matter how brilliant and able and powerful in intellect, in the very meridian of life, animated by an ardent and consuming ambition, struggling as no other man has ever done for the high and brilliant position of candidate for the presidency of the United States, at the hand of this great party; or that old and venerable jurist, who, having filled his years with honor, leaves you his last great decision before stepping from the high place of earthly power into the grave, to appear before his Maker, in whose presence deception is impossible, and earthly position is as dust in the balance?

We simply claim that we, being coequal with you in the Territories, we having property which is as sacred to us as yours is to you, that is recognized as such by the Constitution of our common country—shall enjoy, unmolested, the rights to go into the Territories, and to remain there, and enjoy those rights as citizens of the United States, as long as our common government holds those Territories in trust for the States of which we are citizens. That is all.

We shall go to the wall upon this issue if events shall demand it, and accept defeat upon it. Let the threatened thunders roll and the lightning flash through the sky, and let the dark cloud now resting on the Southern horizon be pointed out by you. Let the world know that our people are in earnest. In accepting defeat upon that issue, my countrymen, we are bound to rise, if there is virtue in the Constitution. But if we accept your policy, where shall we be? We shall then have assented to the great fact involved in adopting your platform, that the government is a failure so far as the protection of the South in the Territories is concerned. We should be estopped for ever from asserting our principle simply by your pointing to the record that we had assented to the fact that the government could not be administered on a clear assertion of our rights. Is it true, gentlemen of the Northwest? Is it true, gentlemen of the whole country, that our government is a failure so far as the plain and unequivocal rights of the South are concerned? If it be a failure, we are not patriots unless we go to work at the very foundation stone of this error and reconstruct this party on a proper basis.

To my countrymen of the South I have a few words here to say. Be true to your constitutional duties and rights. Be true to your own sense of right. Accept of defeat here, if defeat is to attend the assertion of the right, in order that you may secure a permanent victory in whatever contest you carry a constitutional banner. Yield nothing of principle for mere party success—else you will die by the hands of your associates as surely as by the hand of your avowed enemy.

A party, in its noblest sense, is an organized body that pledges itself to the people to administer the government on a constitutional basis. The people have no interest in parties, except to have them pledged to administer the government for the protection of their rights. The leaders of the masses, brilliant men, great statesmen, may, by ever ignoring the people's rights, still have a brilliant destiny in the rewards of office and the distribution of eighty millions annually; but when those leaders, those statesmen, become untrue to the people, and ask the people to vote for a party that ignores their rights, and dares not acknowledge them, in order to put and keep them in office, they ought to be strung upon a political gallows higher than that ever erected for Haman.

JEFFERSON DAVIS

ON WITHDRAWING FROM THE UNION [1]
(1861)

Born in 1808, died in 1889; graduated from West Point in 1828; elected to Congress in 1845; served in the Mexican War in 1846–47; elected United States Senator in 1847; Secretary of War in 1853; United States Senator again in 1857; resigned as Senator in 1861; President of the Confederacy in 1861–65; arrested in May, 1865, and imprisoned until 1867; amnestied in 1868.

I RISE, Mr. President, for the purpose of announcing to the Senate that I have satisfactory evidence that the State of Mississippi, by a solemn ordinance of her people in convention assembled, has declared her separation from the United States. Under these circumstances, of course my functions are terminated here. It has seemed to me proper, however, that I should appear in the Senate to announce that fact to my associates, and I will say but very little more. The occasion does not invite me to go into argument, and my physical condition would not permit me to do so if it were otherwise; and yet it seems to become me to say something on the part of the State I here represent, on an occasion so solemn as this.

It is known to senators who have served with

[1] Delivered in the United States Senate to a crowded audience on January 21, 1861.

me here that I have for many years advocated, as an essential attribute of State sovereignty, the right of a State to secede from the Union. Therefore, if I had not believed there was justifiable cause; if I had thought that Mississippi was acting without sufficient provocation, or without an existing necessity, I should still, under my theory of the government, because of my allegiance to the State of which I am a citizen, have been bound by her action. I, however, may be permitted to say that I do think that she has justifiable cause, and I approve of her act. I conferred with her people before the act was taken, counseled them then that if the state of things which they apprehended should exist when the convention met, they should take the action which they have now adopted.

I hope none who hear me will confound this expression of mine with the advocacy of the right of a State to remain in the Union, and to disregard its constitutional obligations by the nullification of the law. Such is not my theory. Nullification and secession, so often confounded, are indeed antagonistic principles. Nullification is a remedy which it is sought to apply within the Union, and against the agent of the States. It is only to be justified when the agent has violated his constitutional obligation, and a State, assuming to judge for itself, denies the right of the agent thus to act, and appeals to the other States of the Union for a decision;

but when the States themselves, and when the people of the States, have so acted as to convince us that they will not regard our constitutional rights then, and then for the first time, arises the doctrine of secession in its practical application.

A great man who now reposes with his fathers, and who has been often arraigned for a want of fealty to the Union, advocated the doctrine of nullification because it preserved the Union. It was because of his deep-seated attachment to the Union, his determination to find some remedy for existing ills short of a severance of the ties which bound South Carolina to the other States, that Mr. Calhoun advocated the doctrine of nullification, which he proclaimed to be peaceful, to be within the limits of State power, not to disturb the Union, but only to be a means of bringing the agent before the tribunal of the States for their judgment.

Secession belongs to a different class of remedies. It is to be justified upon the basis that the States are sovereign. There was a time when none denied it. I hope the time may come again when a better comprehension of the theory of our government, and the inalienable rights of the people of the States, will prevent any one from denying that each State is a sovereign, and thus may reclaim the grants which it has made to any agent whomsoever.

I therefore say I concur in the action of the people of Mississippi, believing it to be necessary and proper, and should have been bound by their action if my belief had been otherwise; and this brings me to the important point which I wish on this last occasion to present to the Senate. It is by this confounding of nullification and secession that the name of the great man, whose ashes now mingle with his mother earth, has been invoked to justify coercion against a seceded State. The phrase "to execute the laws" was an expression which General Jackson applied to the case of a State refusing to obey the laws while yet a member of the Union. That is not the case which is now presented. The laws are to be executed over the United States, and upon the people of the United States. They have no relation to any foreign country. It is a perversion of terms, at least it is a great misapprehension of the case, which cites that expression for application to a State which has withdrawn from the Union. You may make war on a foreign State. If it be the purpose of gentlemen, they may make war against a State which has withdrawn from the Union; but there are no laws of the United States to be executed within the limits of a seceded State. A State finding herself in the condition in which Mississippi has judged she is, in which her safety requires that she should provide for the maintenance of her rights out of the Union, surrenders all the benefits (and they are known to be many), deprives herself of the advantages (they are known to be great), severs all the ties of affection (and they are close and enduring), which have bound her to the Union; and thus divesting herself of every benefit, taking upon herself every burden, she claims to be exempt from any power to execute the laws of the United States within her limits.

I well remember an occasion when Massachusetts was arraigned before the bar of the Senate, and when then the doctrine of coercion was rife and to be applied against her because of the rescue of a fugitive slave in Boston. My opinion then was the same that it is now. Not in a spirit of egotism, but to show that I am not influenced in my opinion because the case is my own, I refer to that time and that occasion as containing the opinion which I then entertained, and on which my present conduct is based. I then said, if Massachusetts, following her through a stated line of conduct, chooses to take the last step which separates her from the Union, it is her right to go, and I will neither vote one dollar nor one man to coerce her back; but will say to her, Godspeed, in memory of the kind associations which once existed between her and the other States.

It has been a conviction of pressing necessity, it has been a belief that we are to be deprived in the Union of the rights which our fathers bequeathed to us, which has brought Mississippi into her present decision. She has heard proclaimed the theory that all men are created free and equal, and this made the basis of an attack upon her social institutions; and the sacred Declaration of Independence has been invoked to maintain the position of the equality of the races. That Declaration of Independence is to be construed by the circumstances and purposes for which it was made. The communities were declaring their independence; the people of those communities were asserting that no man was born—to use the language of Mr. Jefferson —booted and spurred to ride over the rest of mankind; that men were created equal—meaning the men of the political community; that there was no divine right to rule; that no man inherited the right to govern; that there were no classes by which power and place descended to families, but that all stations were equally within the grasp of each member of the body politic. These were the great principles they announced; these were the purposes for which they made their declaration; these were the ends to which their enunciation was directed. They have no reference to the slave, else how happened it that among the items of arraignment made against George III. was that he endeavored to do just what the North had been endeavoring of late to do—to stir up insurrection among our slaves? Had the Declaration announced that the negroes were free and equal, how was the prince to be arraigned for stirring up insurrection among them? And how was this to be enumerated among the high crimes which caused the Colonies to sever their connection with the mother country? When our Constitution was formed the same idea was rendered more palpable, for there we find provision made for that very class of persons as property; they were not put upon the footing of equality with white men—not even upon that of paupers and convicts; but, so far as representation was concerned, were discriminated against as a lower caste, only to be represented in the numerical proportion of three-fifths. Then, senators, we recur to the compact which binds us together; we recur to the principles upon which our government was founded; and when you deny them, and when you deny to us the right to withdraw from a government which, thus perverted, threatens to be destructive of our rights, we but tread in the path of our fathers when we proclaim our independence, and take the hazard. This is done, not in hostility to others, not to injure any section of the country, not even for our own pecuniary benefit, but from the high and solemn motive of defending and protecting the rights we inherited, and which it is our sacred duty to transmit unshorn to our children.

I find in myself, perhaps, a type of the general feeling of my constituents toward yours. I am sure I feel no hostility to you, senators from the North. I am sure there is not one of you, whatever sharp discussion there may have been between us, to whom I can not now say, in the presence of my God, I wish you well;

and such, I am sure, is the feeling of the people whom I represent toward those whom you represent. I therefore feel that I but express their desire when I say I hope, and they hope, for peaceful relations with you, tho we must part. They may be mutually beneficial to us in the future, as they have been in the past, if you so will it. The reverse may bring disaster on every portion of the country; and if you will have it thus, we will invoke the God of our fathers, who delivered them from the power of the lion, to protect us from the ravages of the bear; and thus, putting our trust in God, and in our firm hearts and strong arms, we will vindicate the right as best we may. I see now around me some with whom I have served long; there have been points of collision; but whatever of offense there has been to me, I leave here; I carry with me no hostile remembrance. Whatever offense I have given which has not been redressed, or for which satisfaction has not been demanded, I have, senators, in this hour of our parting, to offer you my apology for any pain which, in heat of discussion, I have inflicted. I go hence unencumbered of the remembrance of any injury received, and having discharged the duty of making the only reparation in my power for any injury offered.

Mr. President and senators, having made the announcement which the occasion seemed to me to require, it only remains for me to bid you a final adieu.

TOOMBS

ON RESIGNING FROM THE SENATE[1]
(1861)

Born in 1810, died in 1885; elected to Congress in 1845; United States Senator in 1853; resigned in 1861; Member of the Confederate Congress in 1861; Secretary of State in 1861; a Brigadier-General, serving at the second battle of Bull Run and at Antietam; refused to take the oath of allegiance to the United States Government.

THE success of the Abolitionists and their allies, under the name of the Republican party, has produced its logical results already. They have for long years been sowing dragons' teeth and have finally got a crop of armed men. The Union, sir, is dissolved. That is an accomplished fact in the path of this discussion that men may as well heed. One of your confederates has already, wisely, bravely, boldly confronted public danger, and she is only ahead of many of her sisters because of her greater facility for speedy action. The greater majority of those sister States, under like circumstances, consider her cause as their cause; and I charge you in their name to-day: "Touch not Saguntum."[2] It is not only their cause, but it is a cause which re-

---

[1] Delivered in the United States Senate on January 7, 1861.

[2] Saguntum was a city of Iberia (Spain) in alliance with Rome. Hannibal, in spite of Rome's warnings in 219 B.C., laid siege to and captured it. This became the immediate cause of the war which Rome declared against Carthage.

ceives the sympathy and will receive the support of tens and hundreds of thousands of honest patriot men in the nonslaveholding States, who have hitherto maintained constitutional rights, and who respect their oaths, abide by compacts, and love justice.

And while this Congress, this Senate, and this House of Representatives are debating the constitutionality and the expediency of seceding from the Union, and while the perfidious authors of this mischief are showering down denunciations upon a large portion of the patriotic men of this country, those brave men are coolly and calmly voting what you call revolution—aye, sir, doing better than that: arming to defend it. They appealed to the Constitution, they appealed to justice, they appealed to fraternity, until the Constitution, justice, and fraternity were no longer listened to in the legislative halls of their country, and then, sir, they prepared for the arbitrament of the sword; and now you see the glittering bayonet, and you hear the tramp of armed men from your capitol to the Rio Grande. It is a sight that gladdens the eyes and cheers the hearts of other millions ready to second them. Inasmuch, sir, as I have labored earnestly, honestly, sincerely, with these men to avert this necessity so long as I deemed it possible, and inasmuch as I heartily approve their present conduct of resistance, I deem it my duty to state their case to the Senate, to the country, and to the civilized world.

Senators, my countrymen have demanded no
new government; they have demanded no new
Constitution. Look to their records at home and
here from the beginning of this national strife
until its consummation in the disruption of the
empire, and they have not demanded a single
thing except that you shall abide by the Constitution of the United States; that constitutional rights shall be respected, and that justice
shall be done. Sirs, they have stood by your
Constitution; they have stood by all its require-
ments, they have performed all its duties un-
selfishly, uncalculatingly, disinterestedly, until
a party sprang up in this country which endangered their social system—a party which
they arraign, and which they charge before the
American people and all mankind with having made proclamation of outlawry against four
thousand millions of their property in the Territories of the United States; with having put
them under the ban of the empire in all the
States in which their institutions exist outside
the protection of federal laws; with having
aided and abetted insurrection from within and
invasion from without with the view of sub-
verting those institutions, and desolating their
homes and their firesides. For these causes they
have taken up arms.

I have stated that the discontented States of this
Union have demanded nothing but clear, distinct, unequivocal, well-acknowledged constitutional rights—rights affirmed by the highest

judicial tribunals of their country; rights older than the Constitution; rights which are planted upon the immutable principles of natural justice; rights which have been affirmed by the good and the wise of all countries, and of all centuries. We demand no power to injure any man. We demand no right to injure our confederate States. We demand no right to interfere with their institutions, either by word or deed. We have no right to disturb their peace, their tranquillity, their security. We have demanded of them simply, solely—nothing else— to give us *equality, security and tranquillity.* Give us these, and peace restores itself. Refuse them, and take what you can get.

What do the rebels demand? First, "that the people of the United States shall have an equal right to emigrate and settle in the present or any future acquired Territories, with whatever property they may possess (including slaves), and be securely protected in its peaceable enjoyment until such Territory may be admitted as a State into the Union, with or without slavery, as she may determine, on an equality with all existing States." That is our Territorial demand. We have fought for this Territory when blood was its price. We have paid for it when gold was its price. We have not proposed to exclude you, tho you have contributed very little of blood or money. I refer especially to New England. We demand only to go into those Territories upon terms of equality with you, as equals in this great Confederacy, to enjoy the common property of the whole Union, and receive the protection of the common government, until the Territory is capable of coming into the Union as a sovereign State, when it may fix its own institutions to suit itself.

The second proposition is, "that property in slaves shall be entitled to the same protection from the government of the United States, in all of its departments, everywhere, which the Constitution confers the power upon it to extend to any other property, provided nothing herein contained shall be construed to limit or restrain the right now belonging to every State to prohibit, abolish, or establish and protect slavery within its limits." We demand of the common government to use its granted powers to protect our property as well as yours. For this protection we pay as much as you do. This very property is subject to taxation. It has been taxed by you and sold by you for taxes.

The title to thousands and tens of thousands of slaves is derived from the United States. We claim that the government, while the Constitution recognizes our property for the purposes of taxation, shall give it the same protection that it gives yours.

Ought it not to be so? You say no. Every one of you upon the committee said no. Your senators say no. Your House of Representatives says no. Throughout the length and breadth of your conspiracy against the Constitution there is but one shout of no! This recognition of this right is the price of my allegiance. Withhold it, and you do not get my obedience. This is the philosophy of the armed men who have sprung up in this country. Do you ask me to support a government that will tax my property; that will plunder me; that will demand my blood, and will not protect me? I would rather see the population of my native State laid six feet beneath her sod than they should support for one hour such a government. Protection is the price of obedience everywhere, in all countries. It is the only thing that makes government respectable. Deny it and you can not have free subjects or citizens; you may have slaves.

We demand, in the next place, "that persons committing crimes against slave property in one State, and fleeing to another, shall be delivered up in the same manner as persons committing crimes against other property, and that the laws of the State from which such persons flee shall be the test of criminality." That is another one of the demands of an extremist and rebel.

But the nonslaveholding States, treacherous to their oaths and compacts, have steadily refused, if the criminal only stole a negro and that negro was a slave, to deliver him up. It was refused twice on the requisition of my own State as long as twenty-two years ago. It was refused by Kent and by Fairfield, governors of Maine, and representing, I believe, each of the then federal parties. We appealed then to fraternity, but we submitted; and this constitutional right has been practically a dead letter from that day to this. The next case came up between us and the State of New York, when the present senior senator [Mr. Seward] was the governor of that State; and he refused it. Why? He said it was not against the laws of New York to steal a negro, and therefore he would not comply with the demand. He made a similar refusal to Virginia. Yet these are our confederates; these are our sister States! There is the bargain; there is the compact. You have sworn to it. Both these governors swore to it. The senator from New York swore to it. The governor of Ohio swore to it when he was inaugurated. You can not bind them by oaths. Yet they talk to us of treason; and I suppose they expect to whip freemen into loving such brethren! They will have a good time in doing it!

It is natural we should want this provision of the Constitution carried out. The Constitution says slaves are property; the Supreme Court says so; the Constitution says so. The theft of slaves is a crime; they are a subject-matter of felonious asportation. By the text and letter of the Constitution you agreed to give them up. You have sworn to do it, and you have broken your oaths. Of course, those who have done so look out for pretexts. Nobody expected them to do otherwise. I do not think I ever saw a perjurer, however bald and naked, who could not invent some pretext to palliate his crime, or who could not, for fifteen shillings, hire an Old Bailey lawyer to invent some for him. Yet this requirement of the Constitution is another one of the extreme demands of an extremist and a rebel.

The next stipulation is that fugitive slaves shall be surrendered under the provisions of the Fugitive Slave Act of 1850, without being entitled either to a writ of habeas corpus, or trial by jury, or other similar obstructions of legislation, in the State to which he may flee. Here is the Constitution:

"No person held to service or labor in one State, under the laws thereof, escaping into another, shall, in consequence of any law or regulation therein, be discharged from such service or labor, but shall be delivered up on claim of the party to whom such service or labor may be due."

This language is plain, and everybody understood it the same way for the first forty years of your government. In 1793, in Washington's time, an act was passed to carry out this provision. It was adopted unanimously in the Senate of the United States, and nearly so in the House of Representatives. Nobody then had invented pretexts to show that the Constitution did not mean a negro slave. It was clear; it was plain. Not only the federal courts, but all the local courts in all the States, decided that this was a constitutional obligation. How is it now? The North sought to evade it; following the instincts of their natural character, they commenced with the fraudulent fiction that fugitives were entitled to habeas corpus, entitled to trial by jury in the State to which they fled. They pretended to believe that our fugitive slaves were entitled to more rights than their white citizens; perhaps they were right, they know one another better than I do. You may charge a white man with treason, or felony, or other crime, and you do not require any trial by jury before he is given up; there is nothing to determine but that he is legally charged with a crime and that he fled, and then he is to be delivered up upon demand. White people are delivered up every day in this way; but not slaves. Slaves, black people, you say, are entitled to trial by jury: and in this way schemes have been invented to defeat your plain constitutional obligations.

Senators, the Constitution is a compact. It contains all our obligations and the duties of the federal government. I am content and have ever been content to sustain it. While I doubt its perfection, while I do not believe it was a good compact, and while I never saw the day that I would have voted for it as a proposition *de novo*, yet I am bound to it by oath and by that common prudence which would induce men to abide by established forms rather than to rush into unknown dangers. I have given to it, and intend to give to it, unfaltering support and allegiance, but I choose to put that allegiance on the true ground, not on the false idea that anybody's blood was shed for it. I say that the Constitution is the whole compact. All the obligations, all the chains that fetter the limbs of my people, are nominated in the bond, and they wisely excluded any conclusion against them, by declaring that "the powers not granted by the Constitution to the United States, or forbidden by it to the States, belonged to the States respectively or the people."

Now I will try it by that standard; I will subject it to that test. The law of nature, the law of justice, would say—and it is so expounded by the publicists—that equal rights in the common property shall be enjoyed. Even in a monarchy the king can not prevent the subjects from enjoying equality in the disposition of the public property. Even in a despotic government this principle is recognized. It was the blood and the money of the whole people (says the learned Grotius, and say all the publicists) which acquired the public property, and therefore it is not the property of the sovereign. This right of equality being, then, according to justice and natural equity, a right belonging to all States, when did we give it up? You say Congress has a right to pass rules and regulations concerning the Territory and other property of the United States. Very well. Does that exclude those whose blood and money paid for it? Does "dispose of" mean to rob the rightful owners? You must show a better title than that, or a better sword than we have.

What, then, will you take? You will take nothing but your own judgment; that is, you will not only judge for yourselves, not only discard the court, discard our construction, discard the practise of the government, but you will drive us out, simply because you will it. Come and do it! You have sapped the foundations of society; you have destroyed almost all hope of peace. In a compact where there is no common arbiter, where the parties finally decide for themselves, the sword alone at last becomes the real, if not the constitutional, arbiter. Your party says that you will not take the decision of the Supreme Court. You said so at Chicago; you said so in committee; every man of you in both Houses says so. What are you going to do? You say we shall submit to your construction. We shall do it, if you can make us; but not otherwise, or in any other manner. That is settled. You may call it secession, or you may call it revolution; but there is a big fact standing before you, ready to oppose you—that fact is, freemen with arms in their hands.

LINCOLN

I

THE "HOUSE DIVIDED AGAINST ITSELF" SPEECH [1]

(1858)

Born in 1809, died in 1865; began to practise law in 1837; served in the Black Hawk War in 1832; elected to Congress in 1847; the unsuccessful Republican candidate for the United States Senate in 1858; elected President in 1860; issued the Emancipation Proclamation September 22, 1862; reelected President in 1864; entered Richmond with the Federal Army on April 4, 1865; assassinated ten days later.

IF we could first know where we are, and whither we are tending, we could better judge what to do, and how to do it. We are now far into the fifth year since a policy was initiated with the avowed object, and confident promise, of putting an end to slavery agitation. Under the operation of that policy, that agitation not

[1] Delivered at the Illinois Republican State Convention at Springfield, on June 16, 1858, after he had been chosen the party candidate for the United States Senate, as the successor of Stephen A. Douglas. This speech practically initiated the famous debate between Lincoln and Douglas, which followed during the political campaign of that year. The opening paragraph has often been cited as evidence of Lincoln's political prescience and grasp of the situation. Seward's "Irrepressible Conflict" speech bears a remarkable resemblance to it, but Seward spoke four months after Lincoln. Seward was then the foremost man in his party, while Lincoln was almost unknown outside of his own State. The speech of Seward, in consequence, attracted wide attention, while Lincoln's at the time passed almost

only has not ceased, but has constantly augmented. In my opinion, it will not cease until a crisis shall have been reached and passed. "A house divided against itself can not stand." I believe this government can not endure permanently half slave and half free. I do not expect the Union to be dissolved; I do not expect the house to fall; but I do expect that it will cease to be divided. It will become all one thing, or all the other. Either the opponents of slavery will arrest the further spread of it, and place it where the public mind shall rest in the belief that it is in the course of ultimate extinction; or its advocates will push it forward till it shall become alike lawful in all the States, old as well as new, North as well as South. Have we no tendency to the latter condition? Let any one who doubts carefully contemplate that now

unnoticed. Lincoln had taken extraordinary care in the preparation of his speech. Herndon says:

" He wrote on stray envelopes and scraps of paper as ideas suggested themselves, putting them into that miscellaneous and convenient receptacle, his hat. As the convention drew near, he copied the whole on connected sheets, carefully revising every line and sentence. He had studied and read over what he had written so long and carefully that he was able to deliver it without the least hesitation or difficulty. Before delivering it, he invited a dozen or so of his friends over to the library of the State House, where he read and submitted it to them. Some condemned, and not one indorsed it. But it suited my views, and I said: 'Lincoln, deliver that speech as read; it will make you president.' At the time I hardly realized the force of my prophecy. He rose from his chair, and, after alluding to the careful study and intense thought he had given the question, he answered all the objections substantially as follows: 'Friends, this thing has been retarded long enough. The time has come when these sentiments should be uttered, and if it is decreed that I should go down because of this speech, then let me go down linked to the truth—let me die in the advocacy of what is just and right.'"

almost complete legal combination-piece of machinery, so to speak—compounded of the Nebraska doctrine and the Dred Scott decision.

Put this and that together, and we have another nice little niche, which we may, ere long, see filled with another Supreme Court decision, declaring that the Constitution of the United States does not permit a *State* to exclude slavery from its limits. And this may especially be expected if the doctrine of "care not whether slavery be voted down or voted up," shall gain upon the public mind sufficiently to give promise that such a decision can be maintained when made.

Such a decision is all that slavery now lacks of being alike lawful in all the States. Welcome or unwelcome, such decision is probably coming, and will soon be upon us, unless the power of the present political dynasty shall be met and overthrown. We shall lie down pleasantly dreaming that the people of Missouri are on the verge of making their State free, and we shall awake to the reality, instead, that the Supreme Court has made Illinois a slave State. To meet and overthrow that dynasty is the work before all those who would prevent that consummation. That is what we have to do. How can we best do it?

There are those who denounce us openly to their own friends, and yet whisper to us softly that Senator Douglas is the aptest instrument there is with which to effect that object. They wish us to *infer* all, from the fact that he now has a little quarrel with the present head of the dynasty; and that he has regularly voted with us on a single point, upon which he and we have never differed. They remind us that he is a great man and that the largest of us are very small ones. Let this be granted. "But a living dog is better than a dead lion." Judge Douglas, if not a dead lion, for this work, is at least a caged and toothless one.

How can he oppose the advance of slavery? He does not care anything about it. His avowed mission is impressing the "public heart" to care nothing about it. A leading Douglas Democratic newspaper thinks Douglas's superior talent will be needed to resist the revival of the African slave-trade. Does Douglas believe an effort to revive that trade is approaching? He has not said so. Does he really think so? But if it is, how can he resist it? For years he has labored to prove it a sacred right of white men to take negro slaves into the new Territories. Can he possibly show that it is less a sacred right to buy them where they can be bought cheapest? And unquestionably they can be bought cheaper in Africa than in Virginia.

He has done all in his power to reduce the whole question of slavery to one of a mere right of property; and as such, how can he oppose the foreign slave-trade? How can he refuse that trade in that "property" shall be "perfectly free," unless he does it as a protection to the home production? And as the home producers will probably ask the protection, he will be wholly without a ground of opposition.

Senator Douglas holds, we know, that a man may rightfully be wiser to-day than he was yesterday—that he may rightfully change when he finds himself wrong. But can we, for that reason run ahead, and infer that he will make any particular change, of which he himself has given no intimation? Can we safely base our action upon any such vague inference? Now, as ever, I wish not to misrepresent Judge Douglas's position, question his motives, or do aught that can be personally offensive to him. Whenever, if ever, he and we can come together on principle, so that our cause may have assistance from his great ability, I hope to have interposed no adventitious obstacle. But, clearly, he is not now with us—he does not pretend to be, he does not promise ever to be.

Our cause, then, must be entrusted to, and conducted by, its own undoubted friends—those whose hands are free, whose hearts are in the work—who *do care* for the result. Two years ago the Republicans of the nation mustered over thirteen hundred thousand strong. We did this under the single impulse of resistance to a common danger. With every external circumstance against us, of strange, discordant, and even hostile elements, we gathered from the four winds, and formed and fought the battle through, under the constant hot fire of a disciplined, proud, and pampered enemy. Did we brave all then, to falter now?—now, when that same enemy is wavering, dissevered, and belligerent! The result is not doubtful. We shall not fail—if we stand firm, we *shall not fail.* Wise counsels may accelerate, or mistakes delay it; but, sooner or later, the victory is sure to come.

II

ON THE FIRST DEBATE WITH DOUGLAS[1]

WHEN a man hears himself somewhat misrepresented, it provokes him—at least, I find it so with myself; but when misrepresentation becomes very gross and palpable, it is more apt to amuse him. The first thing I see fit to notice is the fact that Judge Douglas alleges, after running through the history of the old Democratic and the old Whig parties, that Judge Trumbull[2] and myself made an arrangement in

---

[1] Delivered at Ottawa, Illinois, August 21, 1858. Abridged. The Nicolay and Hay version, used by permission of the Century Company. This debate occurred during the campaign for the election of the Legislature of Illinois, which should choose a successor to Douglas in the United States Senate. Douglas was returned to the Senate, but this debate gave Lincoln a national reputation, making him an available candidate against Douglas for the presidency in 1860. The arguments which Lincoln forced Douglas to make alienated Southern Democrats from Douglas and so lost him their support for president, Lincoln's election being made possible through the nomination of a second Democratic candidate by the South.

See note to Yancey's speech in the Charleston Convention, on page 192 of this volume.

[2] Lyman Trumbull, United States senator from Illinois, 1855–73, who drafted the Thirteenth Amendment to the Constitution.

1854 by which I was to have the place of General Shields in the United States Senate, and Judge Trumbull was to have the place of Judge Douglas. Now all I have to say upon that subject is that I think no man—not even Judge Douglas— can prove it, because it is not true. I have no doubt he is "conscientious" in saying it. As to those resolutions that he took such a length of time to read, as being the platform of the Republican party in 1854, I say I never had anything to do with them, and I think Trumbull never had. Judge Douglas can not show that either of us ever did have anything to do with them.

Now, about this story that Judge Douglas tells of Trumbull bargaining to sell out the old Democratic party, and Lincoln agreeing to sell out the old Whig party, I have the means of knowing about that; Judge Douglas can not have and I know there is no substance to it whatever. Yet I have no doubt he is "conscientious" about it. I know that after Mr. Lovejoy got into the Legislature that winter, he complained of me that I had told all the old Whigs of his district that the old Whig party was good enough for them, and some of them voted against them because I told them so.

Anything that argues me into his idea of perfect social and political equality with the negro is but a specious and fantastic arrangement of words, by which a man can prove a horse-chestnut to be a chestnut horse. I will say here, while upon this subject, that I have no purpose directly to interfere with the institution of slavery in the States where it exists. I believe I have no lawful right to do so, and I have no inclination to do so. I have no purpose to introduce political and social equality between the white and the black races. There is a physical difference between the two, which, in my judgment, will probably for ever forbid their living together upon the footing of perfect equality; and inasmuch as it becomes a necessity that there must be a difference, I, as well as Judge Douglas, am in favor of the race to which I belong having the superior position.

I have never said anything to the contrary, but I hold that, notwithstanding all this, there is no reason in the world why the negro is not entitled to all the natural rights enumerated in the Declaration of Independence—the right of life, liberty, and the pursuit of happiness. I hold that he is as much entitled to these as the white man. I agree with Judge Douglas he is not my equal in many respects—certainly not in color, perhaps not in moral or intellectual endowment. But in the right to eat the bread, without the leave of anybody else, which his own hand earns, he is my equal and the equal of Judge Douglas, and the equal of every living man.

Now I pass on to consider one or two more of these little follies. The judge is wofully at fault about his early friend Lincoln being a "grocery keeper." I do not know that it would be a great sin if I had been; but he is mistaken. Lincoln never kept a grocery anywhere in the world. It is true that Lincoln did work the latter part of one winter in a little still-house up at the head of a hollow. And so I think my friend, the judge, is equally at fault when he charges me at the time when I was in Congress of having opposed our soldiers who were fighting in the Mexican War. The judge did not make his charge very distinctly, but I tell you what he can prove, by referring to the record. You remember I was an old Whig, and whenever the Democratic party tried to get me to vote that the war had been righteously begun by the president, I would not do it. But whenever they asked for any money, or land-warrants, or anything to pay the soldiers there, during all that time, I gave the same vote that Judge Douglas did. You can think as you please as to whether that was consistent.

Such is the truth; and the judge has the right to make all he can out of it. But when he, by a general charge, conveys the idea that I withheld supplies from the soldiers who were fighting in the Mexican War, or did anything else to hinder the soldiers, he is, to say the least, grossly and altogether mistaken, as a consultation of the records will prove to him.

As I have not used up so much of my time as I had supposed, I will dwell a little longer upon one or two of these minor topics upon which the judge has spoken. He has read from my speech in Springfield in which I say that "a house divided against itself can not stand." Does the judge say it can stand? I do not know whether he does or not. The judge does not seem to be attending to me just now, but I would like to know if it is his opinion that a house divided against itself can stand. If it is, then there is a question of veracity, not between him and me, but between the judge and an authority of a somewhat higher character.

Now, my friends, I ask your attention to this matter for the purpose of saying something seriously. I know that the judge may readily enough agree with me that the maxim which was put forth by the Savior is true, but he may allege that I misapply it; and the judge has a right to urge that in my application I do misapply it, and then I have a right to show that I do not misapply it. When he undertakes to say that because I think this nation, so far as the question of slavery is concerned, will all become one thing or all the other, I am in favor of bringing about a dead uniformity in the various States in all their institutions, he argues erroneously. The great variety of the local institutions in the States, springing from differences in the soil, differences in the face of the country, and in the climate, are bonds of union. They do not make "a house divided against itself" but they make a house united.

If they produce in one section of the country what is called for by the wants of another section, and this other section can supply the wants of the first, they are not matters of discord but bonds of union, true bonds of union.

But can this question of slavery be considered as among these varieties in the institutions of the country? I leave it to you to say whether, in the history of our government, this institution of slavery has not always failed to be a bond of union, and, on the contrary, been an apple of discord and an element of division in the house. I ask you to consider whether, so long as the moral constitution of men's minds shall continue to be the same, after this generation and assemblage shall sink into the grave, and another race shall arise with the same moral and intellectual development we have—whether, if that institution is standing in the same irritating position in which it now is, it will not continue an element of division?

If so, then I have a right to say that, in regard to this question, the Union is a house divided against itself; and when the judge reminds me that I have often said to him that the institution of slavery has existed for eighty years in some States, and yet it does not exist in some others, I agree to the fact, and I account for it by looking at the position in which our fathers originally placed it—restricting it from the new Territories where it had not gone, and legislating to cut off its source by the abrogation of the slave-trade, thus putting the seal of legislation against its spread. The public mind did rest in the belief that it was in the course of ultimate extinction. But lately, I think—and in this I charge nothing on the judge's motives—lately, I think, that he, and those acting with him, have placed that institution on a new basis, which looks to the perpetuity and nationalization of slavery. And while it is placed upon this new basis, I say, and I have said, that I believe we shall not have peace upon the question until the opponents of slavery arrest the further spread of it, and place it where the public mind shall rest in the belief that it is in the course of ultimate extinction; or, on the other hand, that its advocates will push it forward until it shall become alike lawful in all the States, old as well as new, North as well as South. Now I believe if we could arrest the spread, and place it where Washington and Jefferson and Madison placed it, it would be in the course of ultimate extinction, and the public mind would, as for eighty years past, believe that it was in the course of ulitmate extinction. The crisis would be past, and the institution might be let alone for a hundred years—if it should live so long—in the States where it exists, yet it would be going out of existence in the way best for both the black and the white races.

I ask the attention of the people here assembled and elsewhere, to the course that Judge

Douglas is pursuing every day as bearing upon this question of making slavery national. Not going back to the records, but taking the speeches he makes—the speeches he made yesterday, and the day before, and makes constantly all over the country—I ask your attention to them. In the first place, what is necessary to make the institution national? Not war. There is no danger that the people of Kentucky will shoulder their muskets, and, with a young nigger stuck on every bayonet, march into Illinois and force them upon us. There is no danger of our going over there and making war upon them. Then what is necessary for the nationalization of slavery? It is simply the next Dred Scott decision.

It is merely for the Supreme Court to decide that no State under the Constitution can exclude it, just as they have already decided that under the Constitution neither Congress nor the Territorial Legislature can do it. When that is decided and acquiesced in, the whole thing is done. This being true, and this being the way, as I think, that slavery is to be made national, let us consider what Judge Douglas is doing every day to that end. In the first place, let us see what influence he is exerting on public sentiment. In this and like communities, public sentiment is everything. With public sentiment, nothing can fail; without it, nothing can succeed. Consequently he who molds public sentiment goes deeper than he who enacts statutes or pronounces decisions. He makes statutes and decisions possible or impossible to be executed. This must be borne in mind, as also the additional fact that Judge Douglas is a man of vast influence, so great that it is enough for many men to profess to believe anything when they once find out that Judge Douglas professes to believe it. Consider also the attitude he occupies at the head of a large party—a party which he claims has a majority of all the voters in the country.

This man sticks to a decision which forbids the people of a Territory to exclude slavery, and he does so not because he says it is right in itself—he does not give any opinion on that— but because it has been decided by the court, and, being decided by the court, he is, and you are, bound to take it in your political action as law—not that he judges at all of its merits, but because a decision of the court is to him a "Thus saith the Lord." He places it on that ground alone, and you will bear in mind that thus committing himself unreservedly to this decision, commits himself on account of the merit or demerit of the decision, but it is a "Thus saith the Lord." The next decision, as much as this, will be a "Thus saith the Lord." There is nothing that can divert or turn him away from this decision. It is nothing that I point out to him that his great prototype, General Jackson, did not believe in the binding force of decisions. It is nothing to him that Jefferson did not so believe.

But I can not shake Judge Douglas's tooth loose from the Dred Scott decision. Like some obstinate animal (I mean no disrespect) that will hang on when he has once got his teeth fixed—you may cut off a leg, or you may tear away an arm, still he will not relax his hold. And so I may point out to the judge, and say that he is bespattered all over, from the beginning of his political life to the present time, with attacks upon judicial decisions,—I may cut off limb after limb of his public record, and strive to wrench from him a single dictum of the court, yet I can not divert him from it. He hangs to the last to the Dred Scott decision. These things show there is a purpose strong as death and eternity for which he adheres to this decision, and for which he will adhere to all other decisions of the same court. [A Hibernian: "Give us something besides Drid Scott."] Yes; no doubt you want to hear something that does not hurt.

Now, having spoken of the Dred Scott decision, one more word and I am done. Henry Clay—my beau-ideal of a statesman, the man for whom I fought all my humble life—Henry Clay once said of a class of men who would repress all tendencies to liberty and ultimate emancipation, that they must, if they would do this, go back to the era of our independence, and muzzle the cannon which thunders its annual joyous return; they must blow out the moral lights around us; they must penetrate the human soul, and eradicate there the love of liberty; and then, and not till then, could they penetrate slavery in this country! To my thinking, Judge Douglas is, by his example and vast influence, doing that very thing in this community when he says that the negro has nothing in the Declaration of Independence. Henry Clay plainly understood the contrary.

Judge Douglas is going back to the era of our Revolution, and to the extent of his ability muzzling the cannon which thunders its annual joyous return. When he invites any people, willing to have slavery, to establish it, he is blowing out the moral lights around us. When he says he "cares not whether slavery is voted down or voted up"—that it is a sacred right of self-government—he is, in my judgment, penetrating the human soul and eradicating the light of reason and the love of liberty in this American people. And now I will only say that when, by all these means and appliances, Judge Douglas shall succeed in bringing public sentiment to an exact accordance with his own views —when these vast assemblages shall echo back all these sentiments—when they shall come to repeat his views and to avow his principles, and to assent to all that on these mighty questions,—then it needs only the formality of the second Dred Scott decision, which he indorses in advance, to make slavery alike lawful in all the States—old as well as new, North as well as South.

III

HIS FAREWELL WORDS IN SPRINGFIELD[1]
(1861)

My friends, no one, not in my situation, can appreciate my feeling of sadness at this parting. To this place and the kindness of this people I owe everything. Here I have lived a quarter of a century and have passed from a young to an old man. Here my children have been born and one is buried.

I now leave, not knowing when or whether ever I may return, with a task before me greater than that which rested upon Washington. Without the assistance of that Divine Being who

---

[1] Delivered on February 11, 1861, and here given as printed by Nicolay and Hay "from the original manuscript, having been written down immediately after the train started, partly by Mr. Lincoln's own hand and partly by that of his private secretary at his dictation." Herndon gives a somewhat longer and textually different version of the speech, as printed at the time in a Springfield newspaper:

"Friends, no one who has never been placed in a like position can understand my feelings at this hour, nor the oppressive sadness I feel at this parting. For more than a quarter of a century I have lived among you, and during all that time I have received nothing but kindness at your hands. Here I have lived from my youth until now I am an old man. Here the most cherished ties of earth were assumed. Here all my children were born and here one of them lies buried. To you, dear friends, I owe all that I have, all that I am. All the strange checkered past seems to crowd now upon my mind.

"To-day I leave you. I go to assume a task more difficult than that which devolved upon Washington. Unless the great God who assisted him shall be with and aid me I must fail; but if the same omniscient mind and mighty arm that directed and protected him shall guide and support me I shall not fail—I shall succeed. Let us all pray that the God of our fathers may not forsake us now. To Him I commend you all. Permit me to ask that with equal sincerity

ever attended him I can not succeed. With that assistance I can not fail.

Trusting in Him who can go with me and remain with you and be everywhere for good, let us confidently hope that all will yet be well. To His care commending you, as I hope in your prayers you will commend me, I bid you an affectionate farewell.

and faith you will invoke His wisdom and guidance for me. With these words I must leave you—for how long I know not. Friends, one and all, I must now bid you an affectionate farewell."

Nicolay and Hay, both of whom were with Lincoln at the time, describe the circumstances in which Lincoln made the speech:

" Early Monday morning (the 11th) found Mr. Lincoln, his family and suite at the rather dingy little railway station at Springfield, with a throng of at least one thousand of his neighbors who had come to bid him good-by. It was a stormy morning which served to add gloom and depression to their spirits. The leave-taking presented a scene of subdued anxiety, almost of solemnity. Mr. Lincoln took a position in the waiting-room where his friends filed past him, merely pressing his hand in silent emotion. The half-finished ceremony was broken in upon by the ringing bells and rushing train. The crowd closed about the railroad car into which the president-elect and his party made their way. Then came the central incident of the morning. The bell gave notice of starting, but as the conductor paused, with his hand lifted to the bell-rope, Mr. Lincoln appeared on the platform of the car and raised his hand to command attention. The bystanders bared their heads to the falling snowflakes, and standing thus his neighbors heard his voice for the last time, in the city of his home, in a farewell address, so chaste and pathetic, that it reads as if he already felt the tragic shadow of forecasting fate."

IV

THE FIRST INAUGURAL ADDRESS [1]
(1861)

In compliance with a custom as old as the government itself, I appear before you to address you briefly, and to take in your presence the oath prescribed by the Constitution of the United States to be taken by the president "before he enters on the execution of his office."

I do not consider it necessary at present for me to discuss those matters of administration about which there is no special anxiety or excitement.

Apprehension seems to exist, among the people of the Southern States, that by the accession of a Republican administration their property and their peace and personal security are to be

[1] On the morning of inauguration day, March 4, 1861, an anonymous writer, quoted by Herndon, Lincoln's biographer, stood in the crowd at Willard's Hotel, where Lincoln was stopping. He describes how an open barouche drove up and the only occupant stepped out —"a large, heavy, awkward-moving man, far advanced in years, short and thin gray hair, full faced, plentifully seamed and wrinkled, head curiously incline ' to the left shoulder, a low-crowned, broad-brimmed silk hat, an immense white cravat like a poultice thrusting the old-fashioned standing-collar up to the ears, dressed in black throughout, with swallow-tail coat not of the newest style: it was President Buchanan, calling to take his successor to the Capitol." The anonymous writer then describes Lincoln's appearance and manner when he arrived at the eastern portico of the Capitol:

"He wore brand-new clothes; black dress-coat instead of the usual frock; black cloth or satin vest, black pantaloons, and a glossy hat, evidently just out of the box. To cap the climax of novelty, he carried a huge ebony cane with a gold head the size of an egg. In these, to him strange habiliments, he looked so miserably uncom-

endangered. There never has been any reasonable cause for such apprehension. Indeed, the most ample evidence to the contrary has all the while existed and been open to their inspection. It is found in nearly all the published speeches of him who now addresses you. I do but quote from one of those speeches when I declare that "I have no purpose, directly or indirectly, to interfere with the institution of slavery in the States where it exists. I believe I have no lawful right to do so, and I have no inclination to do so." Those who nominated and elected me did so with full knowledge that I had made this and many similar declarations, and had never recanted them. And more than this, they placed

---

fortable, that I could not help pitying him. Reaching the platform, his discontent was visibly increased by not knowing what to do with the hat and cane; and so he stood there the target for ten thousand eyes, holding cane in one hand and hat in the other, the very picture of helpless embarrassment. After some hesitation he pushed the cane into a corner of the railing, but could not find a place for the hat, except on the floor where I could see that he did not like to risk it. Douglas, who fully took in the situation, came to the rescue of his old friend and rival, and held the precious hat until the owner needed it again—a service which, if predicted two years before, would probably have astonished him."

"In the central group of this inauguration ceremony," say Nicolay and Hay, "there confronted each other four historic personages in the final act of a political drama which, in its scope, completeness, and consequences, will bear comparison with those most famous in human record—Senator Douglas, the author of the repeal of the Missouri Compromise, representing the legislative power of the American government; Chief Justice Taney, author of the Dred Scott decision, representing the influence of the judiciary, and President Buchanan, who, by his Lecompton measures and messages, had used the full executive power and patronage to intensify and perpetuate the mischiefs born of the repeal and the dictum." Slightly abridged.

in the platform for my acceptance, and as a law to themselves and to me, the clear and emphatic resolution which I now read:

"*Resolved*, That the maintenance inviolate of the rights of the States, and especially the right of each State to order and control its own domestic institutions according to its judgment exclusively, is essential to the balance of power on which the perfection and endurance of our political fabric depend, and we denounce the lawless invasion by armed force of the soil of any State or Territory, no matter under what pretext, as among the gravest of crimes."

I now reiterate these sentiments; and, in doing so, I only press upon the public attention the most conclusive evidence of which the case is susceptible, that the property, peace, and security of no section are to be in any wise endangered by the now incoming administration. I add, too, that all the protection which, consistently with the Constitution and the laws, can be given, will be cheerfully given to all the States, when lawfully demanded, for whatever cause, as cheerfully to one section as to another.

There is much controversy about the delivering up of fugitives from service or order. The clause I now read is as plainly written in the Constitution as any other of its provisions:

"No person held to service or labor in one State, under the laws thereof, escaping into another, shall, in consequence of any law or regulation therein, be discharged from such service or labor, but shall be delivered up on claim of the party to whom such service or labor may be due."

242

It is scarcely questioned that this provision was intended by those who made it for the reclaiming of what we call fugitive slaves; and the intention of the lawgiver is the law. All members of Congress swear their support to the whole Constitution—to this provision as much as any other. To the proposition, then, that slaves whose cases come within the terms of this clause, ''shall be delivered up,'' their oaths are unanimous. Now, if they would make the effort in good temper, could they not, with nearly equal unanimity, frame and pass a law by means of which to keep good that unanimous oath?

There is some difference of opinion whether this clause should be enforced by national or State authority, but surely that difference is not a very material one. If the slave is to be surrendered, it can be of but little consequence to him, or to others, by what authority it is done. And should any one, in any case, be content that his oath should go unkept, on a mere unsubstantial controversy as to how it shall be kept?

Again, in any law upon this subject, ought not all the safeguards of liberty known in civilized and humane jurisprudence to be introduced, so that a free man be not, in any case, surrendered as a slave? And might it not be well, at the same time, to provide by law for the enforcement of that clause of the Constitution which guarantees that ''the citizens of each State shall be entitled to all privileges and immunities of citizens in the several States?''

I take the official oath to-day with no mental reservation, and with no purpose to construe the Constitution or laws by any hypercritical rules. And while I do not choose now to specify particular acts of Congress as proper to be enforced, I do suggest that it will be much safer for all, both in official and private stations, to conform to and abide by all those acts which stand unrepealed, than to violate any of them, trusting to find impunity in having them held to be unconstitutional.

It is seventy-two years since the first inauguration of a president under our national Constitution. During that period, fifteen different and greatly distinguished citizens have, in succession, administered the executive branch of the government. They have conducted it through many perils, and generally with great success. Yet, with all this scope for precedent, I now enter upon the same task for the brief constitutional term of four years, under great and peculiar difficulty. A disruption of the federal Union, heretofore only menaced, is now formidably attempted.

I hold that in contemplation of universal law, and of the Constitution, the Union of these States is perpetual. Perpetuity is implied, if not expressed, in the fundamental law of all national governments. It is safe to assert that no government proper ever had a provision in its organic law for its own termination. Continue to execute all the express provisions of our national government, and the Union will endure for ever—it being impossible to destroy it, except by some action not provided for in the instrument itself

Again, if the United States be not a government proper, but an association of States in the nature of contract merely, can it, as a contract, be peaceably unmade by less than all the parties who made it? One party to a contract may violate it—break it, so to speak; but does it not require all to lawfully rescind it?

Descending from these general principles, we find the proposition that, in legal contemplation, the Union is perpetual, confirmed by the history of the Union itself. The Union is much older than the Constitution. It was formed, in fact, by the Articles of Association in 1774. It was matured and continued by the Declaration of Independence in 1776. It was further matured, and the faith of all the then thirteen States expressly plighted and engaged that it should be perpetual, by the Articles of Confederation in 1778. And, finally, in 1787, one of the declared objects for ordaining and establishing the Constitution was "to form a more perfect union."

But if destruction of the Union, by one, or by a part only, of the States, be lawfully possible, the Union is less perfect than before, the Constitution having lost the vital element of perpetuity.

It follows, from these views, that no State, upon its own mere motion, can lawfully get out of the Union; that resolves and ordinances to that effect are legally void; and that acts of violence within any State or States, against the authority of the United States, are insurrectionary or revolutionary, according to circumstances.

I therefore consider that, in view of the Constitution and the laws, the Union is unbroken, and to the extent of my ability I shall take care, as the Constitution itself expressly enjoins upon me, that the laws of the Union be faithfully executed in all the States. Doing this, I deem to be only a simple duty on my part; and I shall perform it, so far as practicable, unless my rightful masters, the American people, shall withhold the requisite means, or, in some authoritative manner, direct the contrary. I trust this will not be regarded as a menace, but only as the declared purpose of the Union that it will constitutionally defend and maintain itself. In doing this there need be no bloodshed or violence; and there shall be none, unless it be forced upon the national authority. The power confided to me will be used to hold, occupy, and possess the property and places belonging to the government, and to collect the duties and imposts; but beyond what may be necessary for these objects, there will be no invasion, no using of force against or among the people anywhere. Where hostility to the United States, in any interior locality, shall be so great and universal as to prevent competent resident citizens from holding the federal offices, there will be no attempt to force obnoxious strangers among the people for that object. While the strict legal right may exist in the government to enforce the exercise of these offices, the attempt to do so would be so irritating, and so nearly impracticable withal, that I deem it better to forego, for the time, the uses of such offices.

The mails, unless repelled, will continue to be furnished in all parts of the Union. So far as possible, the people everywhere shall have that sense of perfect security which is most favorable to calm thought and reflection. The course here indicated will be followed, unless current events and experience shall show a modification or change to be proper, and in every case and exigency my best discretion will be exercised, according to circumstances actually existing, and with a view and a hope of a peaceful solution of the national troubles, and the restoration of fraternal sympathies and affections.

That there are persons in one section or another who seek to destroy the Union at all events, and are glad of any pretext to do it, I will neither affirm nor deny; but if there be such, I need address no word to them. To those, however, who really love the Union, may I not speak?

Before entering upon so grave a matter as the destruction of our national fabric, with all its benefits, its memories, and its hopes, would it not be wise to ascertain why we do it? Will you hazard so desperate a step while there is any possibility that any portion of the certain ills you fly from have no real existence? Will you, while the certain ills you fly to are greater than all the real ones you fly from—will you risk the commission of so fearful a mistake?

All profess to be content in the Union, if all constitutional rights can be maintained. Is it true, then, that any right, plainly written in the Constitution, has been denied? I think not. Happily the human mind is so constituted that no party can reach to the audacity of doing this. Think, if you can, of a single instance in which a plainly written provision of the Constitution has ever been denied. If, by the mere force of numbers, a majority should derive a minority of any clearly written constitutional right, it might, in a moral point of view, justify revolution—certainly would if such right were a vital one. But such is not our case. All the vital rights of minorities and of individuals are so plainly assured to them by affirmations and negations, guarantees and prohibitions in the Constitution, that controversies never arise concerning them. But no organic law can ever be framed with a provision specifically applicable to every question which may occur in practical administration. No foresight can anticipate, nor any document of reasonable length contain, express provisions for all possible questions. Shall fugitives from labor be surrendered by national or State authority? The Constitution does not expressly say. May Congress prohibit slavery in the Territories? The Constitution does not expressly say. Must Congress protect slavery in the Territories? The Constitution does not expressly say.

From questions of this class spring all our constitutional controversies, and we divide upon them into majorities and minorities. If the minority will not acquiesce, the majority must, or the government must cease. There is no other alternative; for continuing the government is acquiescence on one side or the other. If a minority in such case will secede rather than acquiesce, they make a precedent which, in turn, will divide and ruin them; for a minority of their own will secede from them whenever a majority refuses to be controlled by such a minority. For instance, why may not any portion of a new confederacy, a year or two hence, arbitrarily secede again, precisely as portions of the present Union now claim to secede from it? All who cherish disunion sentiments are now being educated to the exact temper of doing this.

Is there such perfect identity of interests among the States to compose a new Union, as to produce harmony only, and prevent renewed secession?

Plainly, the central idea of secession is the essence of anarchy. A majority held in restraint by constitutional checks and limitations, and always changing easily with deliberate changes of popular opinions and sentiments, is the only true sovereign of a free people. Whoever rejects it, does, of necessity, fly to anarchy or to despotism. Unanimity is impossible; the rule of a minority, as a permanent arrangement, is wholly inadmissible; so that, rejecting the majority principle, anarchy or despotism, in some form, is all that is left.

Physically speaking, we can not separate. We can not remove our respective sections from each other, nor build an impassable wall between them. A husband and wife may be divorced, and go out of the presence and beyond the reach of each other; but the different parts of our country can not do this. They can not but remain face to face, and intercourse, either amicable or hostile, must continue between them. It is impossible, then, to make that intercourse more advantageous or more satisfactory after separation than before. Can aliens make treaties easier than friends can make laws? Can treaties be more faithfully enforced between aliens than laws can among friends? Suppose you go to war; you can not fight always, and when after much loss on both sides and no gain on either you cease fighting, the identical old questions as to terms of intercourse are again upon you.

This country, with its institutions, belongs to the people who inhabit it. Whenever they shall grow weary of the existing government they can exercise their constitutional right of amending it, or their revolutionary right to dismember or overthrow it. I can not be ignorant of the fact that many worthy and patriotic citizens are desirous of having the national Constitution amended. . . . I understand a proposed amendment to the Constitution—which amendment, however, I have not seen—has passed Congress, to the effect that the federal government shall never interfere with the domestic institutions of the States, including that of persons held to service. To avoid misconstruction of what I have said, I depart from my purpose not to speak of particular amendments, so far as to say that, holding such a provision now to be implied constitutional law, I have no objections to its being made express and irrevocable.

The chief magistrate derives all his authority from the people, and they have conferred none upon him to fix terms for the separation of the States. The people themselves can do this also if they choose, but the executive, as such, has nothing to do with it. His duty is to administer the present government as it came to his hands, and to transmit it, unimpaired by him, to his successor. Why should there not be a patient confidence in the ultimate justice of the people? Is there any better or equal hope in the world? In our present differences is either party without faith of being in the right? If the Almighty Ruler of nations, with his eternal truth and justice, be on your side of the North, or yours of the South, that truth and that justice will surely prevail, by the judgment of this great tribunal of the American people. By the frame of the government under which we live, the same people have wisely given their public servants but little power for mischief, and have with equal wisdom provided for the return of that little to their own hands at very short intervals. While the people retain their virtue and vigilance, no administration, by any extreme of wickedness or folly, can very seriously injure the government in the short space of four years.

My countrymen, one and all, think calmly and well upon this whole subject. Nothing valuable can be lost by taking time. If there be an object to hurry any of you in hot haste to a step which you would never take deliberately, that object will be frustrated by taking time; but no good object can be frustrated by it. Such of you as are now dissatisfied still have the old Constitution unimpaired, and on the sensitive point, the laws of your own framing under it; while the new administration will have no immediate power, if it would, to change either. If it were admitted that you who are dissatisfied hold the right side in this dispute there is still no single good reason for precipitate action. Intelligence, patriotism, Christianity, and a firm reliance on Him who has never yet forsaken this favored land are still competent to adjust in the best way all our present difficulty. In your hands, my dissatisfied fellow countrymen, and not in mine, are the momentous issues of civil war. The government will not assail you. You can have no conflict without being yourselves the aggressors. You have no oath registered in heaven to destroy the government, while I shall have the most solemn one to "preserve, protect, and defend" it.

I am loath to close. We are not enemies, but friends. We must not be enemies. Tho passion may have strained, it must not break, our bonds of affection. The mystic chords of memory, stretching from every battle-field and patriot grave to every living heart and hearthstone all over this broad land, will yet swell the chorus of the Union when again touched, as surely they will be, by the better angels of our nature.

V

THE SPEECH AT GETTYSBURG[1]
(1863)

FOURSCORE and seven years ago our fathers brought forth upon this continent a new nation, conceived in liberty, and dedicated to the proposition that all men are created equal.

Now we are engaged in a great civil war, testing whether that nation, or any nation so conceived and so dedicated, can long endure. We are met on a great battle-field of that war. We have come to dedicate a portion of that field[2] as a final resting-place for those who here gave their lives that that nation might live. It is altogether fitting and proper that we should do this.

But in a larger sense, we can not dedicate—we can not consecrate—we can not hallow this ground. The brave men, living and dead, who struggled here, have consecrated it far above our poor[3] power to add or detract. The world will little note, nor long remember, what we say

---

[1] Delivered at the dedication of the cemetery in Gettysburg, November 19, 1863, after Edward Everett had made the formal speech of the day. Printed here in textual conformity to the copy which Lincoln wrote out in his own hand for a soldiers' and sailors' fair, held in Baltimore in 1864.

[2] The Associated Press report, as taken down in shorthand and printed the day after this speech was delivered, here reads, "We are met to dedicate a portion of it."

[3] The Associated Press version omits "poor."

here, but it can never forget what they did here. It is for us, the living, rather, to be dedicated here to the unfinished work which[1] they who fought here thus far so nobly advanced. It is rather for us to be here dedicated to the great task remaining before us—that from these honored dead we take increased devotion to that cause for which they gave the last full measure of devotion—that we here highly resolve that these[2] dead shall not have died in vain—that this nation, under God, shall[3] have a new birth of freedom and that government of the people, by the people, and for the people, shall not perish from the earth.

VI

THE SECOND INAUGURAL ADDRESS[4]
(1865)

At this second appearing to take the oath of the presidential office, there is less occasion for an extended address than there was at first. Then a statement, somewhat in detail, of a course to be pursued seemed very fitting and proper. Now, at the expiration of four years, during which public declarations have been

---

[1] The Associated Press version reads, "That they have thus far so nobly carried on."

[2] The Associated Press version has "the" for "these."

[3] The Associated Press version reads, "That the nation shall, under God."

[4] March 4, 1865.

constantly called forth on every point and phase of the great contest which still absorbs the attention and engrosses the energies of the nation, little that is new could be presented.

The progress of our arms, upon which all else chiefly depends, is as well known to the public as to myself, and it is, I trust, reasonably satisfactory and encouraging to all. With high hope for the future, no prediction in regard to it is ventured.

On the occasion corresponding to this four years ago, all thoughts were anxiously directed to an impending civil war. All dreaded it; all sought to avoid it. While the inaugural address was being delivered from this place, devoted altogether to saving the Union without war, insurgent agents were in the city seeking to destroy it with war—seeking to dissolve the Union and divide the effects by negotiation. Both parties deprecated war, but one of them would make war rather than let the nation survive, and the other would accept war rather than let it perish, and the war came. One-eighth of the whole population were colored slaves, not distributed generally over the Union, but localized in the Southern part of it.

These slaves constituted a peculiar and powerful interest. All knew that this interest was somehow the cause of the war. To strengthen, perpetuate, and extend this interest was the object for which the insurgents would rend the Union by war, while the government claimed no right to do more than to restrict the Territorial enlargement of it.

Neither party expected for the war the magnitude or the duration which it has already attained. Neither anticipated that the cause of the conflict might cease when, or even before the conflict itself should cease. Each looked for an easier triumph, and a result less fundamental and astounding. Both read the same Bible and pray to the same God, and each invokes His aid against the other. It may seem strange that any men should dare to ask a just God's assistance in wringing their bread from the sweat of other men's faces, but let us judge not, that we be not judged. The prayer of both could not be answered. That of neither has been answered fully. The Almighty has His own purposes. "Woe unto the world because of offenses, for it must needs be that offenses come; but woe to that man by whom the offenses cometh!"

If we shall suppose that American slavery is one of those offenses which, in the providence of God, must needs come, but which having continued through His appointed time, He now wills to remove, and that He gives to both North and South this terrible war as the woe due to those by whom the offense came, shall we discern there any departure from those divine attributes which the believers in a living God always ascribe to Him? Fondly do we hope, fervently do we pray, that this mighty scourge of war may speedily pass away. Yet if God wills that it continue until all the wealth piled by the bondsman's two hundred and fifty years of unrequited toil shall be sunk, and until every drop of blood drawn with the lash shall be paid by another drawn with the sword, as was said three thousand years ago, so still it must be said, that the judgments of the Lord are true and righteous altogether.

With malice toward none, with charity for all, with firmness in the right as God gives us to see the right, let us finish the work we are in, to bind up the nation's wounds, to care for him who shall have borne the battle, and for his widow and his orphans, to do all which may achieve and cherish a just and a lasting peace among ourselves and with all nations.

STEPHEN A. DOUGLAS

IN THE FIRST DEBATE WITH LINCOLN[1]

(1858)

Born in 1813, died in 1861; elected Supreme Court Judge in Illinois in 1841; member of Congress in 1843; United States Senator in 1847 and 1853; reported the Kansas-Nebraska Bill in 1854; had a notable debate with Lincoln in 1858; an unsuccessful candidate against Lincoln in 1860.

PRIOR to 1854 this country was divided into two great political parties, known as the Whig and Democratic parties. Both were national and patriotic, advocating principles that were universal in their application. An old-time Whig could proclaim his principles in Louisiana and Massachusetts alike. Whig principles had no boundary sectional line—they were not limited by the Ohio River, nor by the Potomac, nor by the line of the free and slave States, but applied and were proclaimed wherever the Constitution ruled or the American flag waved over the American soil.

So it was, and so it is with the great Democratic party, which, from the days of Jefferson until this period, has proven itself to be the historic party of this nation. While the Whig and Democratic parties differed in regard to

[1] At Ottawa, Illinois, August 21, 1858. The Nicolay and Hay version, used here by permission of the Century Company.

a bank, the tariff distribution, the specie circular, and the subtreasury, they agreed on the great slavery question which now agitates the Union. I say that the Whig party and the Democratic party agreed on the slavery question, while they differed on those matters of expediency to which I have referred. The Whig party and the Democratic party jointly adopted the compromise measure of 1850 as the basis of a proper and just solution of the slavery question in all its forms. Clay was the great leader, with Webster on his right and Cass on his left, and sustained by the patriots in the Whig and Democratic ranks who had devised and enacted the compromise measures in 1850.

In 1854 Mr. Abraham Lincoln and Mr. Lyman Trumbull entered into an arrangement, one with the other, and each with his respective friend to dissolve the old Whig party on the one hand, and to dissolve the old Democratic party on the other, and to connect the members of both into an Abolition party, under the name and disguise of a Republican party. The terms of that arrangement between Lincoln and Trumbull have been published by Lincoln's special friend, James H. Matheny, Esq., and they were that Lincoln should have General Shield's place in the United States Senate, which was then about to become vacant, and that Trumbull should have my seat when my term expired. Lincoln went to work to abolitionize the old Whig party all over the State, pretending that he was then as good a Whig as ever; and Trumbull went to work in his part of the State preaching abolitionism in its milder and lighter form, and trying to abolitionize the Democratic party, and bring old Democrats handcuffed and bound hand and foot into the Abolition camp. In pursuance of the arrangement, the parties met at Springfield in October, 1854, and proclaimed their new platform. Lincoln was to bring into the Abolition camp the old-time Whigs, and transfer them over to Giddings, Chase, Fred Douglass, and Parson Lovejoy, who were ready to receive them and christen them in their new faith.

I desire to know whether Mr. Lincoln to-day stands as he did in 1854, in favor of the unconditional repeal of the Fugitive Slave Law. I desire him to answer whether he stands pledged to-day, as he did in 1854, against the admission of any more slave States into the Union, even if the people want them. I want to know whether he stands pledged against the admission of a new State into the Union with such a Constitution as the people of that State may see fit to make. I want to know whether he stands to-day pledged to the abolition of slavery in the District of Columbia. I desire him to answer whether he stands pledged to the prohibition of the slave-trade between the different States. I desire to know whether he stands pledged to prohibit slavery in all the Territories of the United States, North as well as South of the Missouri Compromise line. I desire him to answer whether he is opposed to the acquisition of any more territory unless slavery is prohibited therein. I want his answer to these questions. Your affirmative cheers in favor of this Abolition platform are not satisfactory.

I ask Abraham Lincoln to answer these questions in order that when I trot him down to lower Egypt, I may put the same questions to him. My principles are the same everywhere. I can proclaim them alike in the North, the South, the East, and the West. My principles will apply wherever the Constitution prevails and the American flag waves. I desire to know whether Mr. Lincoln's principles will bear transplanting from Ottawa to Jonesboro? I put these questions to him to-day distinctly, and ask an answer. I have a right to an answer, for I quote from the platform of the Republican party, made by himself and others at the time that party was formed, and the bargain made by Lincoln to dissolve and kill the old Whig party, and transfer its members, bound hand and foot, to the Abolition party under the direction of Giddings and Fred Douglass.

In the remarks I have made on this platform, and the position of Mr. Lincoln upon it, I mean nothing personally disrespectful or unkind to that gentleman. I have known him for nearly twenty-five years. There were many points of sympathy between us when we first got acquainted. We were both comparatively boys, and both struggling with poverty in a strange land. I was a school-teacher in the town of Winchester, and he a flourishing grocery-keeper in the town of Salem. He was more successful in his occupation than I was in mine, and hence more fortunate in this world's goods. Lincoln is one of those peculiar men who perform with admirable skill everything which they undertake. I made as good a school-teacher as I could, and when a cabinet-maker I made a good bedstead and tables, altho my old boss said I succeeded better with bureaus and secretaries than with anything else; but I believe that Lincoln always was more successful in business than I, for his business enabled him to get into the Legislature.

I met him there, however, and had sympathy with him, because of the uphill struggle we both had in life. He was then just as good at telling an anecdote as now. He could beat any of the boys wrestling, or running a foot-race, in pitching quoits, or tossing a copper; could ruin more liquor than all the boys of the town together, and the dignity and impartiality with which he presided at a horse-race or fist-fight excited the admiration and won the praise of everybody that was present and participated. I sympathized with him because he was strugling with difficulties, and so was I. Mr. Lincoln served with me in the Legislature in 1836 when we both retired, and he subsided, or became submerged, and was lost sight of as a public man for some years.

In 1846, when Wilmot introduced his celebrated proviso, and the Abolition tornado swept over the country, Lincoln again turned up as a member of Congress from the Sangamon district. I was then in the Senate of the United States, and was glad to welcome my old friend and companion. While in Congress, he distinguished himself by his opposition to the Mexican War, taking the side of the common enemy against his own country; and when he returned home he found that the indignation of the people followed him everywhere, and he was again submerged or obliged to retire into private life, forgotten by his former friends. He came up again in 1854, just in time to make an Abolition or Black Republican platform, in company with Giddings, Lovejoy, Chase, and Fred Douglass, for the Republican party to stand upon.

These two men having formed this combination to abolitionize the old Whig party and the old Democratic party, and put themselves into the Senate of the United States, in pursuance of their bargain, are now carrying out that arrangement. Matheny states that Trumbull broke faith; that the bargain was that Lincoln should be the senator in Shield's place, and Trumbull cheated Lincoln, having control of four or five abolitionized Democrats who were holding over in the Senate; he would not let them vote for Lincoln, which obliged the rest of the Abolitionists to support him in order to secure an Abolition senator. There are a number of authorities for the truth of this besides Matheny, and I suppose that even Mr. Lincoln will not deny it.

Washington, Jefferson, Franklin, Hamilton, Jay and the great men of that day made this government divided into free States and slave States, and left each State perfectly free to do as it pleased on the subject of slavery. Why can it not exist on the same principles on which our fathers made it? They knew when they framed the Constitution that in a country as wide and broad as this, with such a variety of climate, production, and interest, the people necessarily required different laws and regulations; what would suit the granite-hills of New Hampshire would be unsuited to the rice-plantations of South Carolina, and they therefore provided that each State should retain its own Legislature and its own sovereignty, with the full and complete power to do as it pleased within its own limits, in all that was local and not national.

One of the reserved rights of the States was the right to regulate the relations between master and servant, on the slavery question. At the time the Constitution was framed, there were thirteen States in the Union, twelve of which were slaveholding States and one a free State. Suppose this doctrine of uniformity preached by Mr. Lincoln, that the States should all be free or all be slave, had prevailed. What would have been the result? Of course, the twelve slaveholding States would have overruled the one free State, and slavery would have fastened by a constitutional provision on every inch of the American Republic, instead of being left, as our fathers wisely left it, to each State to decide for itself. Here I assert that uniformity in the local laws and institutions of the different States is neither possible nor desirable. If uniformity had been adopted when the government was established, it must inevitably have been the uniformity of slavery everywhere, or else the uniformity of negro citizenship and negro equality everywhere.

We are told by Lincoln that he is utterly opposed to the Dred Scott decision, and will not submit to it, for the reason that he says it deprives the negro of the rights and privileges of citizenship. That is the first and main reason which he assigns for his warfare on the Supreme Court of the United States and its decision. I ask you, are you in favor of conferring upon a negro the rights and privileges of citizenship? Do you desire to strike out of our State Constitution that clause which keeps savages and free negroes out of the State, and allow the free negroes to flow in, and cover your prairies with black settlements? Do you desire to turn this beautiful State into a free negro colony, in order that when Missouri abolishes slavery she can send one hundred thousand emancipated slaves into Illinois, to become citizens and voters, on an equality with yourselves? If you desire negro citizenship; if you desire to allow them to come into the State and settle with the white man; if you desire them to vote on an equality with yourselves, and to make them eligible to office, to serve on juries, and to adjudge your rights,—then support Mr. Lincoln and the Black Republican party, who are in favor of the citizenship of the negro. For one, I am opposed to negro citizenship in any and every form. I believe this government was made on the white basis. I believe it was made by white men for the benefit of white men and their posterity for ever; and I am in favor of confining citizenship to white men, men of European birth and descent, instead of conferring it upon negroes, Indians and other inferior races.

Mr. Lincoln, following the example and lead of all the little Abolition orators who go around and lecture in the basements of schools and churches, reads from the Declaration of Independence that all men were created equal, and then asks how can you deprive a negro of that equality which God and the Declaration of Independence award to him? He and they maintain that negro equality is guaranteed by the laws of God, and that it is asserted in the Declaration of Independence. If they think so, of course they have a right to say so, and so vote. I do not question Mr. Lincoln's conscientious belief that the negro was made his equal, and hence is his brother; but for my own part, I do not regard the negro as my equal, and positively deny that he is my brother or any kin to me whatever. Lincoln has evidently learned by heart Parson Lovejoy's catechism. He can repeat it as well as Farnsworth, and he is worthy of a medal from Father Giddings and Fred Douglass for his Abolitionism. He holds that the negro was born his equal and yours, and that he was endowed with equality by the Almighty, and that no human law can deprive him of these rights which were guaranteed to him by the Supreme Ruler of the universe.

Now, I do not believe that the Almighty ever intended the negro to be the equal of the white man. If He did, He has been a long time demonstrating the fact. For thousands of years the negro has been a race upon the earth, and during all that time, in all latitudes and climates, wherever he has wandered or been taken, he has been inferior to the race which he has there met. He belongs to an inferior race, and must always occupy an inferior position. I do not hold that because the negro is our inferior therefore he ought to be a slave. By no means can such a conclusion be drawn from what I have said. On the contrary, I hold that humanity and Christianity both require that the negro shall have and enjoy every right, every privilege, and every immunity consistent with the safety of the society in which he lives. On that point, I presume there can be no diversity of opinion. You and I are bound to extend to our inferior and dependent beings every right, every privilege, every faculty and immunity consistent with the public good.

The question then arises, what rights and privileges are consistent with the public good? This is a question which each State and each Territory must decide for itself—Illinois has decided it for herself. We have provided that the negro shall not be a slave, and we have also provided that he shall not be a citizen, but we protect him in his civil rights, in his life, his person and his property, only depriving him of all political rights whatsoever, and refusing to put him on an equality with the white man. That policy of Illinois is satisfactory to the Democratic party and to me, and if it were to the Republicans, there would then be no question upon the subject; but the Republicans say that he ought to be made a citizen, and when he becomes a citizen he becomes your equal, with all your rights and privileges. They assert the Dred Scott decision to be monstrous because it denies that the negro is or can be a citizen under the Constitution.

Now, I hold that Illinois had a right to abolish and prohibit slavery as she did, and I hold that Kentucky has the same right to continue and protect slavery that Illinois had to abolish it. I hold that New York had as much right to abolish slavery as Virginia has to continue it, and that each and every State of this Union is a sovereign power, with the right to do as it pleases upon the question of slavery, and upon all its domestic institutions. Slavery is not the only question which comes up in this controversy. There is a far more important one to you, and that is, what shall be done with the free negro? We have settled the slavery question as far as we are concerned; we have prohibited it in Illinois for ever, and in doing so, I think we have done wisely, and there is no man in the State who would be more strenuous in his opposition to the introduction of slavery than I would; but when we settled it for ourselves, we exhausted all our power over that subject. We have done our whole duty, and can do no more. We must leave each and every other State to decide for itself the same question.

In relation to the policy to be pursued toward the free negroes, we have said that they shall not vote; while Maine, on the other hand, has said that they shall vote. Maine is a sovereign State, and has the power to regulate the qualifications of voters within her limits. I would never consent to confer the right of voting and of citizenship upon a negro, but still I am not going to quarrel with Maine for differing from me in opinion. Let Maine take care of her own negroes, and fix the qualifications of her own voters to suit herself, without interfering with Illinois, and Illinois will not interfere with

Maine. So with the State of New York. She allows the negro to vote provided he own two hundred and fifty dollars' worth of property, but not otherwise. While I would not make any distinction whatever between a negro who held property and the one who did not, yet if the sovereign State of New York chooses to make that distinction it is her business and not mine, and I will not quarrel with her for it. She can do as she pleases on this question if she minds her own business, and we will do the same thing.

Now, my friends, if we will only act conscientiously and rigidly upon this great principle of popular sovereignty, which guarantees to each State and Territory the right to do as it pleases on all things, local and domestic, instead of Congress interfering, we will continue at peace one with another. Why should Illinois be at war with Missouri, or Kentucky with Ohio, or Virginia with New York, merely because their institutions differ? They knew that the North and the South, having different climates, productions, and interests, required different institutions. This doctrine of Mr. Lincoln of uniformity among the institutions of the different States, is a new doctrine, never dreamed of by Washington, Madison or the framers of this government. Mr. Lincoln and the Republican party set themselves up as wiser than these men who made this government, which has flourished for seventy years under the principle of popular sovereignty, recognizing the right of each State to do as it pleased.

Under that principle we have grown from a nation of three or four millions to a nation of about thirty millions of people; we have crossed the Alleghany Mountains and filled up the whole Northwest, turning the prairies into a garden, and building up churches and schools, thus spreading civilization and Christianity where before there was nothing but savage barbarism. Under that principle we have become, from a feeble nation, the most powerful on the face of the earth, and if we only adhere to that principle, we can go forward increasing in territory, in power, in strength, and in glory until the Republic of America shall be the north star that shall guide the friends of freedom throughout the civilized world. And why can we not adhere to the great principle of self-government upon which our institutions were originally based? I believe that this new doctrine preached by Mr. Lincoln and his party will dissolve the Union if it succeeds.

END OF VOL. IX